What people are saying about ...

The 10 Myths of Teen Dating

"For parents to understand their daughters better and help them navigate through dating, this book is a must-read."

Kim and Krickitt Carpenter, authors of *The Vow*

"Dating is a cultural reality that is not going away. However, teenagers need guidelines. In *The 10 Myths of Teen Dating*, Dan Anderson gives realistic guidance. I highly recommend this book."

Gary Chapman, PhD, author of *The Five Love Languages*

"The toughest period of parenting is during the teen years. I survived it with my three, but there were days when I wasn't sure. I wish Dan's book had been available twenty-five years ago, but the good news is that it's available now and offers real, commonsense, practical, and road-tested principles of parenting. Don't wait to read it until your kids are sixteen—read it when they are twelve and be prepared!"

Mike Huckabee, former governor of Arkansas, former daily radio host of *The Mike Huckabee Show*, former television talk show host of *1*

"I've written extensively on teenage girls and preparing them for the challenges of sexual integrity. I believe *The 10 Myths of Teen Dating* is an exceptional work to help prepare your daughter for the complexities of the teen dating years. Dan and Jacquelyn's book will open up conversations for you and your daughter that will help her date with maturity and grace."

Shannon Ethridge, MA, life/relationship coach, international speaker, and author of twenty-two books, including *Every Young Woman's Battle*

"I'm the father of a soon-to-be teenage girl. I can't imagine a better book about teenagers and dating. The lessons of *The 10 Myths of Teen Dating* are sure to help any family."

Todd Hoffman, star of Discovery Channel's *Gold Rush*

"*The 10 Myths of Teen Dating* is a crucial book for parents as they guide their girls to become 'smart daters.' This book, written by a wise father, educator, and husband, is filled with information and life lessons. It offers concrete advice on starting conversations that encourage girls to bring self-respect, awareness, and intentionality to their relationships."

Bea Herzberg, over one million Pinterest followers

"Dan is a powerhouse. Every time I'm around him, he's just buzzing with energy and vision and life. But unlike a lot of type-A personalities, he's also dripping with wisdom. This is a man who's been around, and who has become a wise sage. His many years as a father and high school teacher have created the incubator for wisdom to grow and thrive. This man is worth listening to: this book is worth reading."

John Mark Comer, pastor for teaching and vision at Bridgetown Church

"After twelve years of Youth For Christ ministry, twenty years getting my two daughters through adolescence, and twenty-five years pastoring, I wish Dan had written this as many years ago. Dan is writing for our times and our daughters and sons, and I would make this must reading for clergy, rabbis, pastors, parents, and our kids."

Hugh Halter, US director of Forge America

THE 10 MYTHS OF TEEN DATING

THE 10 MYTHS OF TEEN DATING

Truths your daughter needs to know to date smart, avoid disaster, and protect her future

DANIEL ANDERSON MEd
with his daughter JACQUELYN ANDERSON MEd

David C Cook®

transforming lives together

THE 10 MYTHS OF TEEN DATING
Published by David C Cook
4050 Lee Vance View
Colorado Springs, CO 80918 U.S.A.

David C Cook U.K., Kingsway Communications
Eastbourne, East Sussex BN23 6NT, England

The website addresses recommended throughout this book are offered as a
resource to you. These websites are not intended in any way to be or imply an
endorsement on the part of David C Cook, nor do we vouch for their content.

Details in some stories have been changed to protect
the identities of the persons involved.

Scripture quotations marked THE MESSAGE are taken from THE MESSAGE.
Copyright © by Eugene H. Peterson 1993, 2002. Used by permission of
Tyndale House Publishers, Inc. Scripture quotations marked NIV are taken
from the Holy Bible, NEW INTERNATIONAL VERSION®, NIV®.
Copyright © 1973, 2011 by Biblica, Inc.® Used by permission. All rights
reserved worldwide. NEW INTERNATIONAL VERSION® and NIV® are
registered trademarks of Biblica, Inc. Use of either trademark for the offering
of goods or services requires the prior written consent of Biblica, Inc.

LCCN 2016941367
ISBN 978-0-7814-1421-0
eISBN 978-0-7814-1439-5

© 2016 Dan Anderson and Jacquelyn Anderson
Published in association with literary agent Tawny Johnson of D.C. Jacobson &
Associates LLC, an Author Management Company. www.dcjacobson.com.

The Team: Ingrid Beck, Alice Crider, Liz Heaney, Amy Konyndyk,
Nick Lee, Jack Campbell, Susan Murdock
Cover Design: Jon Middel

Printed in the United States of America
First Edition 2016

1 2 3 4 5 6 7 8 9 10

062716

CONTENTS

Foreword

Ever since our book *The Vow* was published we have gotten requests to endorse books and write forewords but we have generally been reluctant to do so. However, something about Dan and Jacquelyn's book appealed to us from the start. Maybe it was how we came to meet them.

Kim was on a beach in Hawaii and spotted Todd Hoffman from the Discovery television show *Gold Rush*. A fan of the show, Kim struck up a conversation with Todd, and soon our families were having dinner together. It was over dinner that Todd mentioned that his brother-in-law Dan was working on a book for parents about their daughters and dating, two topics we have a vested interest in. We asked Dan to reach out to us so we could hear more about the book.

Later that year, Dan and Jacquelyn traveled to our home and we spent many hours together over dinner and bowling and got to know the two of them. What we really appreciate about them is that they are one of the only father-daughter teams we can think of. They write together and work together, and that is unique in our world today. What they have compiled in *10 Myths* are some of the most practical, informative approaches to helping daughters deal with dating that we have ever seen.

We think this book is a must-read for all parents readying their children to enter into the dating stages of their young lives. What a fantastic approach Dan and Jacquelyn have taken to provide an insightful means to understand dating. Their experience as educators interacting with young people makes the book more meaningful and genuine.

What is even more amazing is that although this book was intended to ready young ladies and their families for smart dating, it really has a strong message for anyone in a relationship. Dan and Jacquelyn truly have an excellent understanding of what a healthy dating process encompasses. Even more powerful is how each dating myth is applicable to different people in different phases of relationships.

Because we are parents of a boy and girl who will soon be old enough to date, this book could not have been timed better. We both believe that how our own children date will have a direct impact on the quality of their marriages. We travel all over the world talking about marriage and relationships and see the devastation brought on by failed marriages. We think this book will be a tremendous tool for families to discuss dating and help their daughters make wise choices. We both hope you enjoy what we believe is an exceptional and important book for millions of readers.

Kim and Krickitt Carpenter

Introduction

A Different Kind of Dating Book

In 1971 my sister went on her first date. Because she was the oldest, our entire family was invested in this watershed moment and waited eagerly for her date to arrive. Even though I was only six, I remember it well. Her date pulled up in a VW bus. In typical '70s bus fashion, the windows were all becurtained. As the redheaded boy stepped out of the VW, I thought he looked just like Bernie from the TV show *Room 222*. (You may want to Google image him. Trust me, you don't want to miss the hair.) With a bouncing, white-man 'fro he sauntered to the door, then whisked my sister away. They climbed into the van for the greatest night of my sister's life. "Bernie" turned the key, but the van wouldn't start. He turned it again, and again, all with the same result.

In order for my sister to go on her first date, my father, brother, and I would have to push start the van. So with the mighty effort of two small boys and a paunchy, middle-aged man, we set the vehicle in motion. Soon we were at a run, pushing with all our might. With a pop of the VW's clutch, the bus sputtered and lurched to life. As the bus sped away, its window curtains swayed from side to side, revealing momentary glimpses inside the back—and of a bed, ready to go. I can only imagine what terrors were in my father's mind at that moment. After that van pulled away, and once my father's shock wore off, I wonder if he said to himself, "I hope she is ready for this."

A lot has changed since 1971, but one thing hasn't: it is never too early to start preparing your daughter for the world of dating.

WHY THIS BOOK

I have a question to ask you: Where did you learn about dating? If you are like many parents, your information came from a variety of sources. It may have come from your parents. You certainly learned a great deal from your own dating experiences. Perhaps as an adult you have taken a marriage class or read a book about relationships. Regardless of your sources, I can assure you of one fact: you know way more than your daughter.

Where does your daughter learn about dating? Her resources are scant. Many girls learn about dating by talking to their friends, which is like two first-time parachutists looking to each other for advice as they are leaving the plane. It is a little late to ask the important questions as you plunge toward the ground. Lots of girls get their ideas about dating by watching TV and movies. But mostly young women learn about dating through trial and error. While trial and error may be fine when painting your living room, it's a terrible way to learn about dating, because your future happiness is at stake.

I've been in high schools for over two decades and have observed thousands of teenage dating relationships from the outside looking in. I want to tell you it is not a pretty sight. I've been witness to pregnancies, emotional and physical abuse, unsafe sex, cheating, rebound relationships, and enough teen pain and drama to fill five books. I have talked to girls about their cheating boyfriends. I've talked to boys about their indifferent girlfriends. I've watched from my desk as girls ran out of class in tears. I've eavesdropped on boys' conversations and marveled about how little they know about girls. I have seen more hickeys on necks than I can count on my fingers and toes. I've watched couples argue in the hallways, and I've seen those same couples kissing in the hallways the next day. Over time I've become convinced that dating, as practiced by many teenagers, just isn't any good for them.

About a decade ago I decided I'd had enough and began to teach my students about dating myths that most of them seemed to embrace without question. Initially I shared a few random thoughts that, over time, evolved into a researched body of ideas. One thing has been constant over the years: teens are intrigued by these ideas. They crave information about dating and relationships and don't have good sources of wisdom on the topic. It is from this research, and sharing with thousands of students about dating, that this book began to emerge. Because I have a close relationship with my students, they can think through these ideas and we can discuss them. However, a book written for teenage girls lacks the immediacy of a classroom setting, where students can question and discuss a tough topic.

So, I wrote this book for you, the parent, so that you might engage your daughter in discussions around dating and her future happiness. Your daughter has a set of beliefs and assumptions about dating and relationships. Regardless of what those are, they will impact how she approaches dating and determine whether she will be dating smart or dating dumb. I wrote this book to help you understand what myths she may hold regarding dating and to offer you guidance concerning how you can help her date smart, avoid disaster, and protect her future happiness.

BORN FROM FAILURE

When my oldest daughter, Jacquelyn, was of dating age, I thought I was prepared to guide her into the dating world. After all, hadn't I been teaching teens about dating for a number of years? Hadn't I seen firsthand the mistakes teenagers make? Who better to prepare a daughter for dating than I? As it turns out, almost anyone could have done a better job than I. Though my actions came from a good place in my heart, I bungled the job thoroughly. Because of this, I asked my daughter to coauthor this book with me in order to give you insight into how teenage girls think.

Jacquelyn:
Hello, parents! I'm in my midtwenties and am currently teaching at a high school only a few blocks away from my childhood home. When my dad says that this book was born of failure, he is talking about some of the mistakes he made with me. I certainly don't claim to speak for all teenage girls everywhere, but I can tell you about my experiences and that of my friends. I went to a Christian high school, attended church on Sundays, went to youth group

on Wednesdays, dated Christian boys, and followed Christ myself, yet I still made some big mistakes that I regret. In the upcoming pages, I will offer you some ideas about what might be happening inside your daughter's head along with some suggestions for how to engage with her more effectively regarding these important issues.

Because I did not want my daughter to experience the all-too-often toxic world of teenage dating, my approach was to keep Jacquelyn from dating at all until she turned eighteen. Boy, was that a bad idea! I thought I was protecting her and ensuring that she would get through her teenage years unscathed. And in my defense, it wasn't like I was sending her to a convent. (Though the idea did cross my mind!) My goal was to help her avoid an intimate, exclusive relationship as a teen and all the pitfalls that come with it. So, I discouraged solo dates in favor of group outings. I spent time preaching the dangers of exclusive dating and enforced that idea by saying no to anything that might lead to a serious dating relationship. To Jacquelyn, my dating advice sounded like, "Do we really have to talk about this?" or, "You can date as much as you like when you turn eighteen," or, "Please let the boys in your life know I have a shotgun and am not afraid to use it."

For years I had built my classroom philosophy on changing hearts and minds, not just controlling behavior. I was good at it. But with my own daughter I ignored everything I knew to be true. I was trying to cultivate compliance, when I should have been sowing understanding. I was trying to control behavior, when I should have been shaping Jacquelyn's heart and mind. All my approach did was encourage her to go underground with her dating life; consequently, Jacquelyn had dating relationships that she kept hidden from her mother and me. I forced our daughter to go it alone without the benefit of a parent helping her to navigate the difficult world of teenage dating.

Jacquelyn:

As a teenager, it felt like whenever an adult was talking, the word I heard the loudest was always *no*. In response to my dad's *no* on dating, I ignored his wishes and wandered alone in the dark world of dating from that point on. I had a few boyfriends in high school right under my parents' noses, and I made many of the mistakes outlined in this book. That decision left me with some pain and some regret. I beseech every parent reading this book to avoid the urge to lay down mandates for your daughter in this area and to instead become an agent of education. If my dad had explained and talked through some of the things in this book with me instead of forbidding me to have a boyfriend, I may have been able to avoid much of the pain that I have taken with me from my teenage years.

Because you are reading this I assume that you want your daughter to handle the world of teenage dating with courage, grace, and class. I know I made a number of mistakes as a young man that I want my children to avoid. I'm sure every parent in the world feels the same way. In fact, this is the great challenge of parenting. *How do we raise our kids so that they are better than we are? How do we help them grow up to be independent, moral people who live admirable lives?* In the realm of dating, it should be the goal of every parent that his or her daughter will date in such a way that she is happy both today and well into the future.

I believe that if you teach your daughter about the ten myths of dating, you will have done your part in making this possible. Far too many young women believe these myths to be true. They are progressive in nature, with each one often leading to the next. Most young women will not buy into all ten myths, but many will believe at least some of them. Because there is so much faulty thinking around dating, it is important that you have all the information you can get to help your daughter.

THE BIBLE IS NOT ENOUGH

I want to clarify one thing from the outset: I'm a Christian. There. I said it. And I teach in one of the most liberal high schools on the West Coast—in one of the most liberal cities in America. (Believe me, everything you have seen in the *Portlandia* TV show is spot on.) I swim in a very secular pond, and I see how the non-Christian world looks at the Christian world: with anything from ambivalence to downright hostility. This attitude is often understandable. In many cases the actions of Christians have given biblical teachings a bad name. Through the centuries Christians have often been focused on some issues while ignoring other teachings, such as loving your enemies, social justice, and turning the other cheek. But I believe that both the Hebrew Scriptures and the New Testament have a voice to be heard when it comes to twenty-first-century dating.

While this book leans most heavily on science and research, it does allow the voice of the ancients to speak. There may even be a scripture or two. But strictly speaking, this is not a Christian book or even a book for Christians. It is a book for all parents who want to help their daughters through one of the most difficult phases of their lives—the dating years.

In 1997 the Josh Harris book *I Kissed Dating Goodbye* was released. I was a youth pastor at the time and read the book along with hundreds of thousands of other Christians. Within four years this book had sold over 700,000 copies. But for all that it brought to the discussion of dating, it was limited in its scope to a scriptural look at dating. I think the Christian community often believes that the word *no*, some extra prayer, a few sermons, and the spiritual bromide of Scripture are all that every person needs for a better life.

Don't get me wrong. In a perfect world the teachings of the Bible would be all we need. But we are imperfect people with free will who often choose what we shouldn't despite all that we know and have been told. It is important to add as well that not every Christian shares the evangelical emphasis on scriptural authority. Christianity is a big tent. I believe all parents need something more to help their daughters through the dating years.

I think this something more is what is largely missing from Christian writing on sex and dating—namely, scientific information and practical tools to help your daughter. Not research and thinking to supplant ancient wisdom, but rather new ideas that will engage your daughter's mind and help her clarify her thinking on dating relationships so that it may come in line with timeless wisdom. It's about sowing understanding, not just cultivating compliance.

Regardless of whether you are a Christian, I believe we can all agree that we live in troubling times. Attitudes and behaviors regarding dating and relationships are as dysfunctional and dangerous as they have been at any time in human history. As parents we can't exclude any information that will help us raise our daughters to date smart, avoid disaster, and protect their future happiness.

WARNING: BE PREPARED TO FEEL UNCOMFORTABLE

In order to teach our daughters about dating, we sometimes have to let go of our own assumptions about dating and relationships. This process of letting go of what you think you know about dating promises to be incredibly interesting but just a little bit painful. Let me explain why.

Many years ago, my eleventh-grade economics class and I were having a discussion that somehow became centered on prostitution. One student named Brian was quite insistent that prostitutes choose their fates. The discussion then focused on how much choice a prostitute actually has. What the class agreed on is that *choice* is a difficult word to apply to prostitutes because such a high percentage of them are habitual drug users. Apparently Brian had seen *Pretty Woman* a few too many times, as he then began to argue that prostitutes make a free choice and that in fact most of them are not drug users. It was one thing for Brian to make a philosophic argument about the nature of choice, but quite another to argue that a majority of prostitutes are not habitual drug users. Research suggests that the prevalence of habitual drug use among prostitutes is many, many times that of nonprostitutes.[1] So, in this case, Brian was dead wrong, and I told him so. I said, "Brian, you are dead wrong." Those were my exact words. What happened next I will never forget.

Brian's jaw quite literally dropped for a few moments as he thought of what to say. He was flabbergasted. I wish there were a dramatic flourish to cap this story, but like so many class discussions, the topic veered in another direction and the moment was lost. But it was Brian's gobsmacked expression that remains in my mind's eye.

Just like Brian, you may be taken off guard by some of what you read in this book, because it may challenge your own dating experiences. It may even challenge you in your current relationship. Adults are not immune to unwise relationship patterns and choices. This book relies heavily on research and data that sometimes run counter to what many people believe when it comes to dating and marriage. It is entirely possible that as you read you will find that you have believed some of the dating myths. One of the hardest things to do in life is to accept our own faulty thinking. You may need to do this a few times as you read this book.

The other reason this book may make you uncomfortable is that it may require a 180-degree turn in what you are currently teaching your daughter about dating. As you read the research, learn about the teenage brain, and gain insight from Jacquelyn and other young women about what your daughter may be thinking and what she needs to hear from you, you may realize you need to make some changes in how you are parenting. As you read this book, your jaw may drop from time to time, but I believe you will also gain valuable insight into your dating daughter that will make change inevitable— for both you and her.

OUR CHALLENGE

I will never forget when I first heard the words "Mr. Anderson, what do you think I should do?" I was in my second year teaching in a small town in central Oregon. A girl had come into my class at lunchtime and asked to talk to me. She then proceeded to tell me she was five months pregnant and no one knew except her boyfriend, her best friend, and now me. She had managed to hide her pregnancy from everyone. (It's amazing what a baggy sweater and leather coat can conceal.) After explaining her situation, she said, "Mr. Anderson, what do you think I should do?" That was a big question.

We talked for a very long time that day. We talked about the baby, visiting a doctor, her grades, her boyfriend, and how her family was going to react to the news. Ultimately, she had to answer the question for herself, and it proved to be a difficult forty-eight hours for her. Thankfully, she decided to tell her parents about her pregnancy, and later she gave birth to a healthy baby. She eventually moved with her baby and graduated from high school in another state. Over time I lost track of that student, but what I most remember from that encounter was her question: "What do you think I should do?" This girl's dating behavior had led her down the path to pregnancy. Every parent's nightmare.

Like this student, too many girls date so they are happy in the here and now, but pay a terrible price for that happiness. How can we teach our daughters to date smart today so they can be happy tomorrow? To be happy in both times is equally important. This is the challenge and the focus of this book. It is what I want for my own daughters, and I hope it is what you want for yours.

I believe the most important factors in your daughter's future marital happiness are the ideas, habits, and behaviors about dating that she will put into practice as a teen. It is vital that you have the resources and knowledge to guide her in these formative years. I don't want to equip you for preaching at her, but for communicating with her. Because of this, I want to teach you some crucial things I've learned about teenagers and dating in the past two decades.

Let's dive in!

If I Had a Boyfriend I Would Be Happy

One of the most moving experiences in my life happened soon after my wife and I brought Jacquelyn home from the hospital. Tamara was enjoying some much-deserved rest after a very difficult birth. As I stood in the nursery and held my daughter in my arms, I was overwhelmed, confused, and looking for an owner's manual for this new creation. In that moment I was flooded with unimaginable joy and love. Tears streamed down my face as I felt a surge of emotion for my daughter. The enormous task of rearing a child was washed under by a wave of love in my heart. From this ocean of love flowed every aspiration and dream I had for my daughter. Though years of parenting lay ahead, had you asked me at that moment what I wanted for my daughter in her future, I would have certainly said, "For her to be happy."

I can't imagine any parent alive who doesn't want the same thing for his or her child. In fact, a recent research study conducted across sixty-seven countries suggests that by far the number one wish of parents for their children is that they would be happy.[1] As I said in the introduction, the goal of this book is to help you teach your daughter to date smart today as a way of ensuring her happiness tomorrow. But just what is happiness? How do we obtain happiness? More important, what does your daughter think will make her happy? If she is like many young girls I know, she believes a boyfriend will make her happy.

Jacquelyn:

Being an adolescent girl is strange and hard! As a teen I experienced a constant battle between what I had been taught and knew to be true and what my body was feeling and telling me.

Every summer during my high school years I went with my church youth group to a large Christian conference for teens at a local college. We would stay the week, worship, learn more about God, and spend time with our friends. While that was the surface purpose for the event, the buzzing undertone was that of a mating season. Almost every girl I went to church with—including me—either came to the conference or left the conference with a boyfriend. The bus ride down there was about friendship and the bus ride home was about partnering up with your "beloved." One summer, we got back to the church, and as we were unpacking the bus, a friend of mine burst into tears. She hadn't found a boyfriend and felt as though she would never find one. The look in her tear-filled eyes was of total despair.

While your daughter may not be so extreme in her desire to have a boyfriend, she probably believes that having a boyfriend would make her happier. And it would never occur to her that having a boyfriend might make her life worse.

WHAT IS HAPPINESS ANYWAY?

Though there is no universally agreed-upon definition of happiness, I like the explanation from "Dr. Happiness," Ed Diener. According to Diener, people are happy when they have life satisfaction and more positive emotions than negative ones.[2] I consider myself to be a much happier person than most people, and if I apply this definition to my own life, it fits nicely. Though every life can always be improved, I am content and generally have more positive emotions than negative ones.

So why don't more people experience happiness? According to the Harris Poll in 2011, about 20 percent of Americans rate themselves as unhappy.[3] In a country of enormous wealth and freedom, why are so many dissatisfied with their lives?

I believe it's because people put far too much emphasis on the emotional state of happiness and not enough on life satisfaction. One psychologist even makes distinctions between the *experiencing self* and the *remembering self*.[4] The experiencing self is happy or sad in the very moment that things are happening. While this happiness is fleeting, lasting happiness is ultimately determined by the remembering self. How we look back on our lives is the final arbiter with regard to happiness.

This has certainly been the case for me. Years ago I risked my family's life savings on a building project. Before I could ever get a shovel in the ground, the project appeared dead. In my haste to build a new home for my family, I had left out crucial financing details. (Note to self: the words *left out* and *crucial financing details* should never go together.) I had moved my wife and two young children out of a comfortable home and into a tiny cabin in the woods, where you could literally see the stars through the woodpecker holes in the wall. For many days I agonized over my bad decision and how my family was suffering. I couldn't sleep, eat, or find any peace. I cried for hours on end. Fortunately for my family, I was eventually lucky enough to complete the project and we moved into a new home less than a year later. At the time, my experiencing self was miserable. But my remembering self has an entirely different memory. When I look back on this experience, I see it as one of the most moving, faith-affirming, and defining experiences of my life—one that has contributed enormously to my life satisfaction.

If we view happiness simply as an exercise in balancing the scales of emotional pain and pleasure in the moment, we will ultimately search for happiness in places where it cannot be found. I think many people confuse the short-term state of emotional happiness with the long-term state of life satisfaction, and thus end up looking in the wrong places for happiness. If you want to help your daughter find future happiness, it's important that she—and you—understand where to find genuine, lasting happiness.

But first, let's explore where happiness *is not found.*

YOU'RE LOOKING UNDER THE WRONG ROCK
HAPPINESS IS NOT FOUND IN WEALTH

Studies consistently show wealth does not bring a corresponding rise in happiness. Beyond the initial gains in wealth that pull a person out of poverty, more money doesn't buy more happiness. One significant study claims that after annual household income reaches

$75,000, additional income brings no additional happiness.[5] In his exceptional book *The Progress Paradox*, Gregg Easterbrook observed, "The percentage of Americans who describe themselves as 'happy' has not budged since the 1950s, though the typical person's real income more than doubled through that period."[6]

Another study of individuals with a net worth over $25 million concludes that the superwealthy are in fact unhappy.[7] One writer put it this way: "The respondents turn out to be a generally dissatisfied lot, whose money has contributed to deep anxieties involving love, work, and family. Indeed, they are frequently dissatisfied even with their sizable fortunes. Most of them still do not consider themselves financially secure; for that, they say, they would require on average one-quarter more wealth than they currently possess."[8] If $25 million doesn't buy happiness, I'm fairly certain no amount of money can buy it. Just ask the rich young ruler and the prodigal son.[9] Both of them looked to money and possessions to make them happy. That didn't work out so well for either of them.

As a parent I have always tried to model the idea that happiness is not found in wealth. One concrete way I have communicated this to my children is in the car I drive. For many years, out of economic necessity, I drove some utterly terrible vehicles. I have driven a twenty-year-old Toyota, a thirty-five-year-old VW bus, and a fifteen-year-old Nissan van. (By the way, my mechanic loves me. He sends me a Christmas card every year.) My Nissan van was particularly hideous. As it was our primary vehicle when our children were small, it suffered the variety of indignities—stains, wear and tear, and clumps on the carpet made of who knows what. When I bought Tamara a newer car, I continued to drive the old Nissan. As the scratches, dents, and grime continued to accumulate, my kids would implore me to buy a new vehicle, but I would say, "Just one more year, baby, just one more year." In a now legendary moment in my family's lore, I once took the vehicle in to be detailed. When I picked up the van, the attendant said, "What do you all eat in that car? Waffles?"

Jacquelyn:

We kids were beyond embarrassed to be seen in that van. My mom drove the newer car and always called it the "love car" since it was a gift from her husband. One day we were talking about this idea and my dad pointed out to us that his beat-up, crappy Nissan van was actually the love car. While we were going to awesome summer camps and taking piano lessons, my dad was puttering around town in a rusty bucket with four wheels.

I continued to drive that van well beyond its shelf life for a few reasons. One, it kept me humble. Only a big shot drives a fancy car, and I never want to think of myself as a big shot. But more important, I wanted to communicate to my children in a tangible way that possessions have nothing to do with happiness.

HAPPINESS IS NOT FOUND IN YOUTH

In a surprising and counterintuitive finding, researchers have discovered that happiness throughout life has a U-shaped bend. We are most happy around the age of twenty-three and get progressively less happy until our midforties. One would think that as we age and deteriorate and the warm blood of our youth begins to cool, we would get progressively less happy. However, something curious happens in our forties: we get happier, so much so that happiness peaks again in our mideighties, matching the happiness of our youth. As we get older, we become less capable and watch those around us pass away; yet we are the happiest in our lives.[10]

HAPPINESS IS NOT FOUND IN FAME

In a culture obsessed with all things celebrity we have made an idol out of our idols. Countless television shows, blogs, websites, and magazines glamorize the famous. But one only has to look at the other side of celebrity to see that fame does not bring happiness. From Amy Winehouse to Cory Monteith to Heath Ledger to Philip Seymour Hoffman to Robin Williams, we have seen in recent years that fame is not a buffer against unhappiness. Beyond that, research suggests that chasing extrinsic goals such as wealth and fame actually "related positively to indicators of ill-being."[11]

Jacquelyn:
Even though my parents talked to me about it, this concept was a hard pill for me to swallow as a teen. Like most adolescents, I cared about how people saw me—my identity centered on public opinion. One of the reasons I wanted a boyfriend in high school was that being in a relationship made me "known." Having a boyfriend made me part of a unit, higher up on the social scale. People looked at me, talked about me, noticed what was going on. Here's an

example of what I am talking about. I used to sit next to a pretty popular girl in PE class. Every morning we girls chitchatted about the day's activities. I was usually just a participant, but the day after I got my first boyfriend, I was magically at the center of the conversation. I will never forget it! My friends literally turned, formed a circle around me, and asked me questions about how he had asked me out, what we did when we hung out, how it was going. It was as if having a boyfriend made it so that I now had something to say, some juicy morsel to share. Be aware of this social pressure, particularly if you have a daughter who is actively dating or looking for a boyfriend. A small part of the happiness she gets from this relationship is about fame, being known in her community.

HAPPINESS IS NOT FOUND IN A ROMANTIC RELATIONSHIP

For quite some time scientists believed all people had a set point for their level of happiness. Much like the set point for body weight, which makes dieting exceedingly difficult, researchers used to believe happiness had a predetermined level that changed very little. The latest thinking indicates that our happiness level is more changeable than originally thought.

Sonja Lyubomirsky's recent study, which built on previous twin studies, suggests that about 50 percent of our happiness level is genetically determined and 10 percent is a result of the circumstances in our lives. The remaining 40 percent can be changed through our habits and thinking.[12] Here's how this translates to the teenage girl who believes a boyfriend will be a panacea for her unhappiness. Because 60 percent of her happiness is already set, if she places her happiness in having a boyfriend, the level of happiness she could obtain is far less than the bliss she likely imagines. Even if she has a perfect and amazing relationship (which isn't going to happen), the other 60 percent—genetics and circumstances—will still factor into her overall happiness level. It is safe to say that even in the best of circumstances, a boyfriend will contribute only a little to a girl's happiness.

Jacquelyn:

Two acronyms that represent strong forces that played in my teen life, and were detrimental to my happiness, were FOMO and YOLO. Ever heard of those? FOMO stands for "fear of missing out," a fear that is greatly attributable to social media. You see your friends doing fun things, happy and in love, and you don't want to miss out on that. My junior year of high school, I convinced myself that because I was single I didn't want to go to the Spring Fling Swing Dance. Two texts from a girlfriend on the day of the event later, and I forced my mom to hit the mall and get me a last-minute outfit. I wasn't about to be left out! FOMO can make your daughter feel that she has to have a date to prom, she has to walk down the hall holding her boyfriend's hand, and she will get invited to do fun things with other couples only if she is part of a couple.

YOLO is the idea that "you only live once." In high school I once saw a boy jump off the roof of a house into a pool while shouting, "YOLO!" This thinking was part of why I didn't want to wait until I was eighteen to date. All my friends were dating, and life was passing me by—I wanted to experience all that I possibly could. I really felt like I was getting left behind, not part of the journey that high school had to offer me. Why not try to experience it all?

Parents, just be advised that this is the kind of pressure that is rolling around in your daughter's brain, whether she is aware of it or not. I spent much of my teenage years responding to urges like this.

THE LIMITATIONS OF TEEN ROMANCE

For a teenage girl to look for happiness in a teenage boy makes about as much sense as me looking to my dog to solve a math problem. Don't get me wrong; I like my dog. A lot. She likes to spend time with me. She is always affectionate. She is friendly and really fun to hang out with. But in spite of all this, my dog is no help with my math problems. And a teenage boy is just not mature enough to know how to contribute to anyone's happiness—let alone a teenage girl's. If you are a husband, you probably know that we men are not always good at helping our wives be happy, even with the wisdom of age and experience on our side. This being the case, how much of a chance do teenage boys have of making our daughters happy?

But lack of maturity is not the only reason a boy won't be able to give your daughter the happiness she longs for. Research shows that something else is at play. It's actually the same reason wealth and fame don't bring happiness: *hedonic adaptation*.[13] From the

Greek word *hedone*, which means "pleasure," hedonic adaptation is the process by which pleasurable things become less pleasurable.[14] Simply put, hedonic adaptation is the idea that the intensity of your first experience doing something cannot be repeated. Each successive time you experience something, it becomes slightly less satisfying. While some sensations such as the taste of good food and sex (and drug use, unfortunately) adapt more slowly, many others quickly become mundane because of hedonic adaptation. This also explains why wealth and what it buys do not bring happiness. A car can only be new for so long. Flying first class becomes the norm as we experience it again and again. (But I'd be willing to put that theory to the test by flying first class a few times!) A large house is a thrill when you first walk in, but it soon becomes just another possession. In short, we grow used to the trappings money can buy. The same is true of fame. While the thrill of attention is great, its draw weakens as one becomes accustomed to the feeling.

I have experienced hedonic adaptation as a public speaker. The first time I spoke to a large crowd at a high school graduation, I was nervous but found the experience exhilarating. When every eye is on you and every ear listening, it is a feeling like no other. When you hear the applause, it is as good as any drug. However, as I have spoken to large crowds in the years since, it has become less nerve-racking and less exciting. I'd like to think I've grown more mature and don't need the attention to know I am valuable. But I suspect this is also the work of hedonic adaptation.

So will a boyfriend make your daughter happy? The answer is yes, but only a little bit and only for a little while. This finding is based on the biology of love. Research scientist Helen Fisher posits that love has three stages.[15] The first stage is lust. (We'll look at the other two stages in the dating myth #3 chapter.) The wild, passionate feelings of lust in the early days, weeks, and months of a relationship are incredible, but as they are experienced more and more, they lose some of their potency because of hedonic adaptation. Many young girls confuse the euphoric feelings that accompany this stage with happiness. It certainly seems that one is happier in the early stages of a relationship. However, this emotion fades over time.

We can have that special feeling only for so long before it becomes routine. The writer of the book of Ecclesiastes knew all of this millennia ago when he declared, "Everything is meaningless." Before the era of science, the Hebrew Scriptures warned that happiness is elusive. So given all the places and ways we can't find happiness, just where will your daughter (and you!) find lasting happiness?

FINDING TRUE AND LASTING HAPPINESS

Martin Seligman suggests that happiness has three dimensions: the pleasant life, the good life, and the meaningful life. The pleasant life is closely related to the happiness of the experiencing self, which we discussed earlier. According to Seligman, managing day-to-day emotions and savoring the experiences of life are the first step in happiness. A deeper stage of happiness is found in the good life, which Seligman believes comes from building relationships with others, identifying and using your strengths, and using those strengths in a creative and engaging manner. He goes on to say that the deepest dimension of happiness comes through the meaningful life.[16]

Perhaps the most important element in experiencing a meaningful life is finding a larger purpose for your life. When I think about the happiest people I know, they are those with strong connections to other people and a deep conviction of purpose in their lives. They can clearly articulate their mission in life—and most often it is tied to something much larger than they are. This type of happiness is deeply rewarding, but hard to obtain.

I've worked with thousands of students over the past couple of decades and have been fortunate to teach many brilliant, insightful, and mature young people. But the average teenager isn't capable of identifying with Seligman's three levels of happiness just yet. Because of this I favor a simpler definition of happiness for teenagers. For the young I think the happy life is a rich, goal-centered life.

Jacquelyn:
Despite some dating mistakes, I had a really tremendous and awesome teenage experience. I graduated high school with a tight-knit group of friends, a wealth of experiences, and a great education. What I know now that I didn't know then is that my parents sort of tricked me into having this. If left to my own devices, I can only imagine where I would be. I was, for all intents and purposes, a very happy teenager.

Think about your daughter's strengths. How can you invest in and foster those strengths? Think about your daughter's weaknesses. How can you help her develop those areas? To me, that is what teenage happiness is all about: having a community of people to love and support you in your weaknesses and cherish and celebrate your strengths.

What is the rich life? The rich life is one that has a broad spectrum of experiences out of which a teenager develops a sense of identity and well-being. The modern American ethos in parenting is often hyperfocused on a small number of activities. Parents sign up their kids for lessons in piano or dance or soccer or volleyball or track and so forth. Others want their teens to focus on academics to ensure entrance into a good college. My own son was a high school basketball player, and one June his basketball schedule included twenty-eight games. Twenty-eight games in thirty days! Talk about obsessive. Too many American families have bought into the idea that our value as humans comes from what we do and how well we do it. Many parents believe they are providing the rich life for their children with hyperfocus on a single activity. But what they are really providing is the busy life.

The busy life and the rich life are two very different things. The rich life is more broadly balanced and features academics, sports, the arts, service, travel, spiritual development, and more. The whole person is developed through the rich life. The teenagers I've admired most over the years were those who had a broad base of experience from which they gained their identities. A former student named Olivia comes to mind. Olivia played sports growing up, was active in her church community, volunteered at outdoor school and the local Humane Society shelter, and was the student body president her senior year. All this while maintaining a rigorous class schedule and being one of the most kindhearted and happy students I've ever known. Conversely, the teenagers who have the least satisfying and happy lives are those who are often hyperfocused on one activity or who lead mundane lives in front of the TV, video game console, or cell phone screen. Living a goal-centered life is fundamental to happiness for a teenager. Each human being needs to have a purpose, and when we live out that purpose, it provides richness and meaning.

Many years ago I used to take my excess household garbage to a dumpster next to a motel in my neighborhood. I had permission to dump my overflow garbage there, but each time I opened the lid, Mr. Fred Fox would come out of his room. He was a short, wiry man in his eighties. With a ruddy face and bulbous nose, he questioned me about the nature of my garbage and reminded me that people weren't supposed to dump their trash there without permission. Fred had lived in the same small, squalid apartment for decades. The motel was full of unhappy people who were one step from homelessness. Most of them suffered from addictions, mental health issues, and the malaise that comes from grinding poverty. Fred didn't seem to have many friends or acquaintances other than the employees of the motel, and I don't believe he ever traveled or got out much. But he had a purpose. Though his goal in life was small—to keep people from dumping garbage without permission—it was still a goal. In an otherwise dreary and isolated existence, Mr. Fox's goal of protecting the dumpster sustained him and gave him dignity.

I would like all of our children to have larger goals than protecting a dumpster, but this story illustrates the importance of having a larger purpose.

Jacquelyn:
One of my goals in high school was participating in choir at various levels. I loved to sing, and the community my

school choir provided me with was one that I cherish to this day. My parents supported me in this goal by telling me that I could do it. Even though my dad can't carry a tune in a bucket, he went to hours of choir competitions and rehearsals and listened to me talk about things that he didn't understand. Both of my parents spent their evenings listening to me practice, going to my performances, and driving me to voice lessons. They asked me about how choir was going and I couldn't wait to tell them.

If we want to prepare our daughters for future happiness, we must help them set goals and establish a sense of purpose. In the absence of goals and aspirations, our daughters may find meaning from whatever is in front of them. This is all too often found in a boy. I have discovered over years of teaching that the girls who put too much emphasis on having a boyfriend are the same girls who put far too little emphasis on having a goal-centered life. In many ways a rich, goal-centered life is a buffer against your daughter trying to find happiness in a boyfriend.

So what can you do and say to help your daughter seek happiness in the right places rather than in the wrong places?

PREPARING YOUR DAUGHTER FOR FUTURE HAPPINESS
START EARLY

Being proactive is crucial from the earliest days of your daughter's dating life. One of the most important things you can do is encourage her to ask herself the following questions: *Why do I want to date? What do I hope to accomplish by having a relationship? What am I expecting from a boy when I am in a relationship?* Rather than reacting to her feelings (or her interest in a boy she is already dating), help your daughter clarify her thoughts on dating, ideally before she ever starts dating.

ENCOURAGE HER TO INVEST IN HER OWN INTERESTS AND PASSIONS

Jacquelyn:

One thing I have always appreciated about my parents is that they constantly got behind me. As a teenager I felt like I could try anything because I knew they would support me and find a way to make it happen. Some of my fondest memories are of car rides with my parents to horseback-riding lessons or volleyball tournaments. My dad and I once drove all the way to Reno and back for a volleyball tournament. We talked every single minute of that twelve-hour trip. He told me stories from his child-hood and asked me questions about my life. He even got tickets to see a Shakespeare play on the way down.

What is your daughter interested in? How can you come around her, support her, and make her feel cher-ished in accomplishing her goals? For example, if she is interested in architecture, you might go on a walk down-town and look at some old buildings and talk about them with her. Does she like to draw? If so, you might sit down with her and ask her about what she is working on, what she is thinking.

ENCOURAGE GOAL SETTING

Every year, I teach my students how to write SMART goals, which I find extremely effective. One of the things you can do to help your daughter experience a rich and full life is to encourage her to make some SMART goals—specific, measurable, attainable, realistic, and timely goals—for what she wants to accomplish each year. Be they in nature academic, athletic, musical, spiritual, service related, or otherwise, a healthy set of goals and aspirations can provide interest, focus, and passion to your daughter's life. Help her set SMART goals, then get behind her. Your daughter wants nothing more than to feel supported by you in her endeavors. While you may not always understand, try to listen and do what you can to help her get where she wants to be.

During Jacquelyn's senior year Tamara and I sat down with her and talked about where she saw herself. She said she wanted to participate in vocal competitions at the statewide level and hoped to earn a vocal scholarship for college. Then, the three of us made a plan for what she needed to do to reach her goals.

CREATE OPPORTUNITIES FOR SERVICE

One of our family mantras is "See a need and fill it." Tamara and I said this often to our children. We tried to foster an environment in which service and charity to others were encouraged—and we intentionally tried to model those things. We tried to be generous with our emotions, money, and time for others. I coached our children's sports teams, our family tithed regularly, we took in a foster child, we bought uniforms for their sports teams at school, and we supported their friends when they were having hard times. We did our best to live out the family mantra.

Jacquelyn:

I watched my parents give of their time and money, which in turn helped me do the same when I became an adult. It might have seemed to my parents that I wasn't paying attention, but I was soaking it all up like a sponge. Your daughter is too!

In high school, I helped my mom paint and decorate a few classrooms around the private school where she was an administrator. We would sneak in over the weekend, and the teacher would have a beautiful space to teach in come Monday morning. At dinner my dad often talked about different ways he was giving his time and money to help a student get what he or she needed. My parents created a family commitment to service.

WATCH THE MOVIE HAPPY WITH HER

The exceptional documentary *Happy*, directed by Roko Belic, examines happiness across many cultures and seeks to discover how true happiness is found. It vividly illustrates how material wealth has nothing to do with happiness and offers an excellent opportunity for you to begin a discussion with your daughter on happiness.

ASK HER WHY SHE WANTS TO DATE AND WHAT SHE HOPES TO GET OUT OF DATING

Have this discussion frequently, as your daughter's thoughts on this will change as she gets older.

Jacquelyn:

A significant downside to my going underground about my boyfriends was that my parents and I never talked about the boys I was dating, so I missed the benefit of their wisdom and insights. If they had asked me why I wanted to date in high school, that question would have been a good start to a conversation I really needed to have. I'm sure my answer would have been illuminating both to me and to my parents. Like most teens, I often did things without taking the time to think deeply about why I was doing them.

I believe that if you take the time to talk to your daughter it may help her be more cautious and avoid disaster. I can think of quite a few mistakes I may have not made had my parents encouraged me to stop and think about what I was doing. Unfortunately they often talked *at* me and *to* me but rarely *with* me. Focus on talking *with* your daughter. When she starts asking about going out on dates, ask her why she wants to date. If she doesn't respond immediately, wait a bit. Rephrase your question, or ask a different question entirely.

Instead of asking, "Why do you want a boyfriend?" try asking, "What do you think a boyfriend will add to your life?" Talk with her another time and ask again—and then wait for her to answer. Don't try to fill in the blank or come up with the answer. Listen to her answer, then respond.

As you step into these conversations about some touchy issues, remember that your daughter is amazingly perceptive.

Jacquelyn:
It is crazy how the slightest change in my parents' posture, tenor of voice, or gaze spoke volumes to me when I was a teenager. If they were uncomfortable talking about a topic, I always knew it. So go ahead and acknowledge if you feel a bit awkward and tell your daughter that you are standing behind her, ready to help her navigate the world of dating. Your honesty is about ten times more productive than sidestepping the issues. By setting a tone of honesty and vulnerability, you increase your chances of getting that same honesty and vulnerability from her in return. Some of my best talks with my mom were those in which she shared with me some of her own mistakes. She was always frank, candid, and open for discussion.

THE BOTTOM LINE

True happiness lies with the thoughts in our heads. Having a rich, goal-centered life helps us to be happy. Being connected and committed to something larger than ourselves helps us to be happy. If a girl is miserable and the thoughts in her head are ugly and depressing, having arm candy won't change those thoughts for very long. In the final summation, a relationship is only a complement to the happiness of a person—it does not complete it.

QUESTIONS FOR REFLECTION

1. What have you taught your daughter about where happiness is found?
2. To what extent do you base your own happiness on possessions?
3. How much do you complain? What about? Research suggests that happiness—like a virus—is contagious.[17]

QUESTIONS FOR YOU AND YOUR DAUGHTER TO DISCUSS

1. Have you ever seen a girl who is always looking for a boyfriend? Why do you think she is doing that?
2. From what you know about boys, do you think it is realistic to think that they could make a girl happy? Why or why not? Why would a girl think a boyfriend could make her happy? Are these realistic expectations of boys?
3. What is the danger of being reliant on a relationship to be happy? What can happen when that relationship ends?
4. What are the things in life that make you happiest? How can we (your parents) help you do these things?

LOOKING AHEAD TO THE NEXT CHAPTER

Despite what we understand about happiness, many girls see a boyfriend as the elixir for their unhappiness. As a girl places trust in the boy, in the relationship, and in the "happiness" it brings, she often finds herself in a relationship that becomes increasingly consuming and important to her. Because these dating myths are progressive, with one myth leading to the next, in time she may begin to believe dating myth #2: *I should trust my feelings.*

I Should Trust My Feelings

As a kid growing up in the 1970s, I consumed a steady diet of *Star Trek* reruns. I spent hours lying on the floor, eating cereal, and watching the crew of the USS *Enterprise*. Spock always intrigued me. In my mind he was an A-list celebrity for many reasons. It was not enough that he had the Vulcan mind meld, but he also had the nerve pinch. He had pointy ears and had mastered the Vulcan lute. He could make a laser from his transponder and could navigate the treacherous waters of *pon farr*, a recurring time in his life that demanded he mate or die. Spock was my hero. But he had one other admirable quality. He operated on pure logic and suppressed his emotions. In the immortal words of Mr. Spock, "Logical decision, logically arrived at."[1] In a rapidly changing era, he was the symbol of a soon-to-be bygone era when the rationality of the Enlightenment gave way to the emotional dictates of a postmodern world.

If I were a child growing up today, I would be far more likely to identify with Captain Kirk. Be it in the original TV series, or the recent Hollywood movies, James Tiberius Kirk is a complex character who operates much of his life on the demands and impulses of his emotions. Though the captain admires the rationality of Mr. Spock, he values his own emotional instincts. As Kirk himself said,

"We humans are full of unpredictable emotions that logic cannot solve."[2] The trust Captain Kirk places in his feelings mirrors that of a generation of young people who have been taught to follow their hearts. If I have seen one change in teens over the years I have been teaching, it is the degree to which young people eschew rationality for emotion. It seems as though we are teaching them to place far too much emphasis on their feelings and too little emphasis on their thinking. As a result, today's girls are more likely than ever to live out dating myth #2: *I should trust my feelings.*

THE VAMPIRE DIARIES, REALITY TV, AND FOLLOWING YOUR HEART

When I tell teenage girls they cannot trust their feelings, I get curious looks. This idea is counter to everything they see and hear in popular culture. Consider the television show *The Vampire Diaries*. This is one of my wife's favorite shows. She rarely misses an episode, which means I rarely miss an episode; although, mostly I watch disinterestedly and hope something blows up so that I might be able to stay awake. However, I have gleaned enough in my semi-comatose state to know that in episode after episode, the characters follow their hearts. Their on-again, off-again relationships seem to be never ending. The affairs, breakups, and new loves ebb and flow from season to season, all devoid of any rational thought. Yet, *The Vampire Diaries* has been nominated for dozens of Teen Choice awards over the years and continues to be one of the top-rated TV shows for young women. What is the consistent message of this show? Who you choose to be with in a romantic relationship has nothing to do with rational thought. It's an emotional choice, based on feelings alone, pure and simple.

Jacquelyn:
When I was growing up, my girlfriends and I loved watching all Disney princess films. I watched them so many times I had many of the lines memorized. In high school, my friends and I would sing all the classic songs at the tops of our lungs on our way home from volleyball games. While embarrassing to admit now, this is a testament to the impact these movies have on the girls who watch them. In a nutshell, this is what these movies taught me:

1. Your happy ending means having someone to love.
2. Follow your heart and you will end up where you're supposed to be.
3. Talking animals are always around the corner.

Kidding about the animals, but I bought into the concept of following my heart hook, line, and sinker. Consequently, I often went with my heart because I didn't understand that my heart can't be trusted. I sometimes did things that I shouldn't have because I felt like my heart was leading me toward those decisions.

Educators have also played a role in perpetuating this myth. In recent years we have bolstered self-esteem, sought inclusion, emphasized creative writing, promoted tolerance, preached pluralism, encouraged a day of silence, and fought against bullying. These efforts encourage students to feel first and think second. While having a more kind and understanding society is a good thing, it seems to this teacher that the balance has tipped too much in favor of emotions. If you need any more convincing, just consider the movement on college campuses toward trigger warnings and safe spaces. I think we may have gone too far in respecting the feelings of young people.

Most teenage girls have a difficult time getting their heads around the concept that emotions are fallible. There is cultlike belief that they should follow their hearts as they begin to date. I hear a great deal of "But, Mr. Anderson, you don't understand!" When I ask girls to explain why they can trust their emotions, they usually respond with such self-evident gems as "You have to follow your heart." Or "I have a gut feeling." Or "If you overthink a situation you'll ruin it." While in some cases these things may be true, girls who believe this myth overlook a greater truth: *feelings are fallible and should always be balanced against rational thought.*

Let's examine what science has to say about why your daughter's emotions aren't always trustworthy, so that you will be able to communicate these same truths to your daughter.

WHY SHE SHOULDN'T TRUST HER EMOTIONS
HER BRAIN VALUES SOCIAL BONDING ABOVE ALL ELSE

One reason she can't trust her emotions is because her developing brain is wired to value social bonding above everything else. In her book *The Female Brain*, Louann Brizendine explained that "connecting through talking activates the pleasure centers in a girl's brain." She elaborated that when a teenage girl is talking about things related to romance and sex, the girl receives a "major dopamine and oxytocin rush."[3] Both dopamine (a neurotransmitter) and oxytocin (a neurohormone) make social bonding pleasurable, which in turn makes a teenage girl seek out more social bonding.

This desire for social bonding extends into the dating world. Dopamine and oxytocin levels will also increase during the early stages of a dating relationship. Oxytocin is often called the love hormone because it facilitates bonding and trust between partners. Elevated levels of dopamine and oxytocin can cause your daughter to get carried away with her emotions at the beginning of a relationship.

Every year, I have a few female students for whom learning holds absolutely no interest. It is not that these girls struggle to learn or are not bright, but they find their social world far more engaging than anything the classroom has to offer. When in class, they want to text or talk to friends. The idea of studying at lunch rather than hanging out with friends is unthinkable. Their evenings are not consumed with homework but rather with texting, Facebook, Snapchat, and Instagram. For these girls, the emotional subtext of their social lives is all-consuming. While this type of girl may be the exception and not the rule, the truth remains that teenage girls are wired for social bonding. And in the economy of social bonding, emotions are like money. In the same way we measure wealth by the amount of money we possess, a teenage girl's "wealth" is very much measured by her emotional satisfaction; and in this economy, there isn't always room for rational thought.

Jacquelyn:

I can testify to this! In high school, I had nearly every class with my best friend, Sarah, and we talked through a large percentage of a given class period. We wrote notes and blatantly talked while the teacher was talking. Then we would talk all through lunch. Then we would talk all through whatever after-school practice we had that day. Then we would call each other at night to talk on the phone. I wish I could say this has changed as I have grown up, but I routinely call my group of close girlfriends to go over the events of the day. I cannot stress how true this has been for me and the lives of nearly all the young women I know.

HER BRAIN IS STILL DEVELOPING

Another reason teenage girls often lack emotional objectivity is because their brains are not fully developed. Until a young woman is in her late teens or early twenties, the process of connecting the emotional centers of the brain to the prefrontal cortex is incomplete.[4] Why is this important? Because the prefrontal cortex is the area of the brain that controls impulses and helps regulate emotions. In a teenage girl the connections between the emotional center and the cognitive prefrontal cortex are slow and unreliable. As a result, your teen daughter is unable to fully process her emotions like she will be able to do later in life. This also helps explain why she may have such strong emotional reactions to issues you see as trivial. She does not yet have the ability to regulate her emotions.

I once had a student who was a textbook case of the inability to control her emotions. Each day at school she struggled to remain levelheaded. An innocent look from someone was likely to rouse an over-the-top response from her. Several times she stormed out of my classroom in anger over her grade, and she was also involved in physical altercations with other students. On one occasion in physical education class she became so upset with the classroom aide that she punched him—all 6'2" and 200 pounds of him! No matter how many discussions I had with this student about her behavior, she could not understand that it was wrong. Her defense for her actions was always "He [or she] made me mad." All that mattered was how the person had made her feel.

Your daughter may not be that volatile, but she too lacks a balance between cognitive processes and emotion. Ideally, a person has a healthy balance between emotion and reason. But for a young girl with a developing brain, this balance just isn't there. One researcher put it this way: "Without the fast connection to the prefrontal cortex, big downloads of emotional impulses often result in immediate, raw behaviors and circuit overload."[5] How do I interpret this finding? A teenage girl cannot fully trust her emotions.

SHE MAY HAVE INACCURATE INFORMATION

When I was twelve years old, my father took my brother and me to Seattle to view the King Tut exhibit. In order to get in, we had to wait in a very, very long line. After several hours we finally got to the front of the line and purchased our tickets, but we wouldn't be admitted into the exhibit for several more hours, so sweet freedom was now at hand. I was ready to get out of the line, which stretched for blocks, and explore the city. So I felt confused when my father purchased five tickets. One for me, one for my brother, one for Dad, and two for …? Why had he bought five? I learned the answer soon enough.

My dad proceeded to walk toward the back of the line. All I wanted to do was leave this boredom for the adventures of Seattle. With each step I grew more frustrated and impatient. By the time we reached the back of the line, I was nearly in tears. My emotions were boiling over. Then my father took the two extra tickets and gave them to the last person standing in line. Talk about a paradigm shift. Whereas before I was frustrated and angry, I now felt pride in my father and joy for the lucky folks who had been saved from the torture of standing in line for hours. Because I had incomplete information, my emotional response to what was happening had been inappropriate.

Likewise, when our daughters have the wrong information about a boy they like, their emotional response to him is unreliable. What makes this scenario exceedingly thorny is the fact that when it comes to dating, everybody lies, sometimes intentionally, sometimes unintentionally. When you are dating, you put your best foot forward, right? Numerous studies show that when initially dating someone, both males and females employ deception strategies. In fact, most research suggests males and females use deceptive tactics at similar rates. According to one study that examined online dating profiles on various dating sites, 81 percent of the people had lied on their profiles. This same study concluded people were deceptive about their height, weight, and age. And unsurprisingly, the most common deception involved their profile photos.[6] Another study reports that women commonly stretch the truth when it comes to physical beauty and that men are more likely to be deceptive about their emotional qualities and financial resources.[7]

Jacquelyn:

My high school days were just before the outset of social media in earnest. Today, kids have about ten different ways to get in contact with each other. When I was in school, everyone was on Myspace. You could set your top eight friends, design your profile, even pick a song to play when people visited your page. One of my best girlfriends spent the better part of a year talking and texting a "boy" she met on Myspace. (He was actually thirty-five years old!) She thought it was true love. But it's not just predatory men who lie about themselves in order to get a girl's attention. High school boys can lie too. Sometimes, in an effort to put his best foot forward, a boy goes too far and misrepresents who he truly is.

Researcher David Buss discovered a tendency in college boys to depict "themselves as kinder, more sincere, and more trustworthy than they really are."[8] In another study, researchers asked college boys to view a profile of a girl and then prepare a self-description to submit to her for a possible date. They were told this self-description would be pooled with several others and then the girl would be asked to select one boy for a date. As you may have already guessed, there was no date, but there were some interesting results. What they discovered was that the young men fudged their self-descriptions in order to meet the perceived needs of the potential date. Additionally, the more attractive and desirable the girl, the greater the level of deception. (If you have an exceptionally beautiful daughter—the type who could be a model or an actress—you should make her aware of this.) In the words of the study, many young men "behave in chameleon-like fashion during dating initiation, strategically and deceptively changing their self-presentation in an attempt to appear more desirable to the person they want to date."[9]

So just what do these studies teach us? As a father I'm wired to see boys as the enemy, and so with Jacquelyn I viewed my role as that of a military field general whose job was to "kill" the enemy before he got near the frontlines of my daughter's heart.

Jacquelyn:

I love the intention behind my dad's military general tactics, but I would have benefited much more if he hadn't taken such a hard-line approach. My parents did a great job of setting the stage for dating, for talking about what kind of guy I should be interested in, but because they didn't know about any of my boyfriends, their observations were always in generalities. What they said seemed like a picture that was out of focus, and I didn't really take it to heart.

I definitely had some blind spots when it came to truly seeing the boys I was dating. I could have used my parents' help in holding up a microscope, so to speak, to the boys I was viewing as potential boyfriends. I wish they had had an honest discussion with me that slyly highlighted some truths that I was overlooking about some of the boys I dated. Emphasis on *slyly* here. If they had said flat out that they didn't like a boy I liked, that might have driven me closer to the guy! Be clever here, parents! How can you help your daughter come to her own conclusions?

While they are not the enemy, the fact remains that many teen boys do employ deceptive tactics in order to get the girl. The possibility of deception, along with a teenage girl's inability to smoothly integrate cognitive and emotional functions, makes it even more unwise for a girl to "follow her heart." Not only might a boy be deceiving her about who he is, but her still-developing brain and lack of life experience might also cloud the truth.

What does this research on deception say to me? We should tell our daughters that in the very early stages of a relationship, they should believe half of what they feel and half of what boys say.

SOMETIMES HER PAST UGLIES UP THE PRESENT

There is one more reason why our daughters, or anyone else for that matter, shouldn't trust their emotions. Years ago I heard a sermon simply entitled "This Is Not That." It was one of the finest teachings I'd ever heard from a pastor. In this message he urged his listeners to not let the past pollute the present.

This has been difficult at times in my own life. Some of my earliest memories were of arguments between my parents when I was a child. As a sensitive lad, I was often left confused and hurt by their altercations. I learned that conflict must be like the conflict I saw.

Lots of yelling, screaming, and swearing. I also learned that there is no discussing a problem as it will always lead to a horrible scene. As I've grown older that feeling has never completely gone away. Even today I tend to be nonconfrontational and will do anything to avoid an argument.

My ugly feelings were exposed one afternoon about a decade ago when I was under some extreme pressure. I was teaching full time, general contracting a custom home, coaching high school golf, acting as a youth pastor, raising three children, and working hard to be a good husband. One afternoon it all came crashing down on me. I found myself on my bed, curled up in the fetal position, sobbing and wailing uncontrollably, full of emotional pain. I cried out that I was stupid. Worthless. Ugly. A waste. A disappointment and a failure. A terrible husband and father. It was the lowest point of my life. (I later learned I had experienced what psychologists call a dissociative episode.) When looked at through a rational lens, everything I said in those moments of extraordinary pain was absolutely false. I am not stupid. I am not worthless. I am not ugly (I'm a solid "5," by the way). I am not a waste. I am not a disappointment. I am not a failure. I am not a terrible husband and father. Yet that was how I felt.

No matter how old I've gotten, the wounds from my past often cause me pain in the present. Psychologists call this *transference*. As the name implies, we transfer our feelings from some past event to something happening at the current moment. Transference can happen in our teen years too, which means a girl's emotional reaction to a boy may have as much to do with something in her past as with the boy. That being the case, do we really think it is a good idea to encourage our daughters to trust their hearts and abandon reason? I don't think so.

Over the years I have been teaching, I have discovered that one group of girls in particular drags their past wounds into the present— girls without the day-to-day presence of a father in their lives. Research on fatherless daughters confirms that these girls struggle emotionally and often have difficulty managing relationships.

EMOTIONS AND FATHERLESS DAUGHTERS

Fatherlessness can take many forms. A girl can be fatherless because she never had a father figure in her life; she can be fatherless because of the daily absence of her father as a result of divorce; and she can be fatherless because her father, while living with her, is cold, distant, and not engaged. If you are raising a fatherless daughter, I do not in any way want to be a voice of condemnation. Moms in fatherless families bravely fight every single day for a good life for their children, and my hat is off to each and every one of them. That being said, if you are raising a daughter who has little or no relationship with her father, let's acknowledge a few of the challenges you face.

The first is that your daughter was supposed to have a father in her life, and no matter what you do, there is likely to be some fallout from this: her past will pollute her present. The benefits of having an involved father are well documented. Children with involved fathers have greater cognitive ability and academic proficiency. They are more secure, more resilient, and better able to adapt to new situations. Additionally, they have a superior social competence and maturity. Children with involved fathers also demonstrate better self-control and impulse management as well as a greater sense of empathy.[10] One author identified impulse control and empathy as master emotional skills.[11] These two emotional skills keep us from hurting ourselves and others. More often than not, a girl with an involved father has greater emotional well-being.

At the risk of painting with a very broad brushstroke, I submit that girls from fatherless homes are far more likely to overinvest emotionally in a romantic relationship. In general, my experience as a classroom teacher has shown that the most unhealthy and emotionally off-kilter relationships often involve a girl from a fatherless home. Research backs up my observations, showing that girls from fatherless homes are more likely to marry as teens, get pregnant before marriage, have children as teens, and have higher divorce rates.[12] This does not mean every girl from a fatherless home will suffer from these setbacks. What it does mean is they are at risk for emotionally turbulent and immature relationships. I have seen girls from fatherless homes act out their pain in the following ways:

- Seeking out relationships with deeply flawed boys.
- Seeking male validation and recognition through sexual promiscuity.
- Dating older men.

If you are the mom of a fatherless daughter, I encourage you to work hard to help her minimize the risks with a few specific steps. First, keep your dating life private from your daughter until she is grown up and out of the house. This may mean you have to be single for a very long time. Too often girls from fatherless homes watch their mothers go from relationship to relationship, which can influence their outlook on dating. If she sees you seeking validation from men, what is the lesson she takes to the dating world? Probably the lesson that she is good only if she has a man in her life. This lesson is doubly learned by having an uninvolved father. Many girls from fatherless homes internalize a sense of shame about not having a dad. They try to "fix" this shame by having a man in their lives. If their mothers date, this behavior may only reinforce this idea.

Also, some single mothers live vicariously through their daughters and are happy to see their daughters in dating relationships. I hate even saying it, but I've seen it time and again in my years as a teacher. Perhaps they are hoping the daughter will be saved the pain of loneliness, or perhaps the daughter's relationship meets some need for the mom. In any case, if you are a single mom who wants to help your daughter date smart, be careful you don't push her to date. By pushing her to date, you just may be encouraging her to water a weed.

Second, work hard to put off your daughter dating for as long as possible. The longer she waits to enter the dating world, the better. This will allow time for her brain to mature so it can smoothly integrate the cognitive and emotional processes. The younger she dates, the sooner she will begin to hardwire dating behaviors that may not be healthy.

Third, help your daughter understand the risks and pitfalls of being a fatherless girl. You are not branding your daughter with a "scarlet letter," but you are helping her to understand the reality that fatherless daughters face. A good place to start would be to watch, along with your daughter, the 2013 *Oprah's Lifeclass* episode entitled "Daddyless Daughters."

Finally, help your daughter cultivate a strong relationship with a responsible man: a grandfather, uncle, or close family friend. A daughter without a father needs to see what a healthy marriage looks like, understand how a loving husband treats his wife, and experience the validation of an adult male. Another man can never replace your daughter's father, but he may help your daughter in ways you can't even imagine.

Jacquelyn:

I am alarmed by the number of times I've heard guys talk about girls with "daddy issues." In these guys' minds, a girl with daddy issues is what my mom calls "low-hanging fruit." Easy to reach and easy to get. It is no secret with young men who have devious intentions that damaged women are easy prey. Girls with "daddy issues" are at a higher risk to become that prey.

Of course, having an involved father is no guarantee that a girl will make rational decisions when it comes to dating. What thought or idea will keep a girl's emotions in check when her emotions are saying something completely different? As a parent, I want my daughters to trust their hearts only when that trust is balanced against a degree of rationality. I think the most effective way to create that balance is to have a reference point for thinking rationally. And the best one I know is a firm understanding of her own value.

AN INCREDIBLY POWERFUL REALIZATION

Between 2005 and 2013 I drove a heavily used Chrysler Town and Country mommy van that my family called the "Golden Rocket." When I valued the car, I could take it on a night out with my wife. I could transport my children and their friends without embarrassment or shame. I got the most out of this vehicle because I valued it. But like the Nissan minivan I talked about in the previous chapter, the Golden Rocket also became a pile of junk. Its Kelley Blue Book value plummeted, and at some point the car became worthless. Because I did not feel the car had value, I stopped protecting it. I didn't drive carefully, stopped waxing it, and let major dents go without repair. And I stopped investing in it. Other than oil changes and routine maintenance to keep me from dying in a fiery crash, I did not spend one penny on it. New struts? Why bother. Back into a mailbox while pulling out of your driveway? No problem. Radio broken? Who cares. Air-conditioning out? Use the two-sixty-five method. (You know, two windows and sixty-five miles an hour.) Because I did not feel the car had value, I no longer maximized its utility. And one day it finally happened. I was taking a shortcut down an unpaved road filled with potholes and driving too fast when—*bam!* The Golden Rocket bottomed out with enough force to kill my onboard computer and turn my car into a gigantic paperweight.

Enter a new car. For the first time in my life I was driving a brand-new vehicle: a modest Nissan Versa, perhaps the least expensive new car in America. I chose it solely on the basis of the intersection of gas mileage and the ability to hold my 6'6-1/2" frame. It is surprisingly roomy and has now earned the family nickname of "mini-minivan."

But I saw this car as valuable. I was now keenly interested in protecting my vehicle. I purchased heavy-duty floor mats to protect the carpets. I didn't allow anyone to eat anything—including waffles—in my new car, ever. I invested in my car by scheduling it routinely for maintenance and oil changes. And I maximized the use of my car by once again driving my wife on dates and taking my children places. Because I saw value in this car, I protected it, invested in it, and maximized it.

I see a similarity between how I treated the Golden Rocket and the mini-minivan and how the teen girls I work with each day treat themselves. Some of them believe they are valuable and protect, invest in, and maximize themselves; others do not believe they are valuable and consequently engage in defeatist and often self-destructive behaviors. I have become convinced that few ideas are more powerful than an understanding that one is valuable.

Believing you have value is different from having self-esteem. Self-esteem is a vacuous notion built on nothing. An egregious example of this is a sign that hung above a mirror in an Alabama elementary school bathroom that read, "You are now looking at one of the most special people in the whole wide world!"[13] Self-esteem seeks to promote inner happiness at all costs, whereas human value is grounded in the belief that all human beings have worth and dignity. Self-esteem grows the weed of self-centeredness (I deserve to feel good about myself), whereas human value cultivates inner reflection and self-control. Self-esteem leads to selfishness because to feel good about yourself at all times requires that you become the most important being in the universe. When self-esteem becomes your most important goal, life is one big selfie with no one to photobomb your picture.

However, when you understand that each person has value (and not just you!), it puts other people into your universe and confers on them equal importance with you. Many religions teach that humans are valuable. As a Christian, I believe that all people are valuable because they are created in the image of God, *imago Dei*. In the ancient world only the king or ruler was said to be "in the image of God." But both rabbinic writing and Christian theology promote the notion that we are all made in God's image.[14] One could rightly argue that the Enlightenment and all that came with it are rooted in the belief that all humanity is the *imago Dei*. This belief is the cornerstone philosophy on which human rights and the Declaration of Independence are built. Much of the good of Western civilization is rooted in the *imago Dei*.

The belief that others are equally important fosters empathy, courtesy, and understanding. When you know you are valuable, you will protect yourself rather than act recklessly in a search to feel good. You will invest in yourself, which typically means making painful sacrifices for your own future rather than living in the moment to feel happy. You will maximize yourself, and by that I mean you will make the most of your talents and gifts. My oft-repeated mantra to my students and my own children has become "Protect, invest, and maximize."

Some time ago I was talking with one of my students who was estranged from her family. Her father was heavy handed, and the communication in her family had broken down completely. This student earned good grades, was responsible in her personal life, and by and large made many good choices. However, her parents had asked her to leave the home because she wouldn't comply with what seemed to me to be unfair demands. She was now secretly living in her friend's basement, and her parents had no plan to bring her back home.

I asked her, "How does this all make you feel?"

"I feel stupid and worthless. Like people don't love me," she responded through ever-increasing tears.

I knew that what she needed was a confirmation of her own value. To help make my point, I decided to draw a picture. In my best stick-figure-quality art I drew a pile of dog poop. I showed her the picture and said to her, "You are not a steaming pile of crap. You are a valuable person." Whoa. Point made.

She instantly broke down in tears and cried for a very long time. She told me how she had been feeling worthless, and the estrangement from her family had only made it worse. We talked a great deal more that day, but one thing was clear. She had a new understanding of herself. Though this girl's story is still being written, I hope that a belief in her own value can sustain her. (You'll be happy to know that two years after she and I had this discussion she was carrying a 3.8 GPA in college and was seeking counseling to help rebuild her sense of worth.)

Sadly, this girl is not alone in her feelings. There are so many people who do not understand their own value. When a girl believes she is valuable, she will develop emotional stability. She will possess an inherent dignity. Because she knows everyone else is valuable too, she will be empathetic toward others. And, importantly, she will have the foundation she needs to date smart. She will be far less likely to go places she should not go or do things she should not do. A girl who understands her value will never allow herself to be mistreated, abused, or taken advantage of in a relationship. A girl who understands that she is valuable will date in such a way that she will never stop investing in herself and always seek to make the most of her own talents and gifts. It is when she loses sight of her own value that she begins to compromise her own worth. Her understanding of her value is a defense against blithely embracing many of the dating myths of this book.

Girls who don't understand they are valuable experience a variety of feelings they should not trust. When they don't believe they have value, they act as if the past is best forgotten and the future holds no hope. All that matters is the here and now. They are often racked by self-loathing and insecurity, and their behaviors reflect this. They do not protect themselves and are frequently engaged in a variety of risky behaviors. They do not invest in themselves, and they allow others to take from them. They throw away much of their potential, chasing relationships that will ultimately leave them disappointed. Worst of all, they have few limits on the places they will go emotionally and physically. When the here and now is all that matters, a young girl is prone to make some bad choices. And often these choices are grounded in an overreliance on her own emotions. Because of this, our role as parents should be to help our daughters balance emotions with rational thinking. And with that goal in mind, let's look at some specific things you can do.

PREPARING YOUR DAUGHTER FOR FUTURE HAPPINESS
CREATE A CLIMATE OF RATIONAL THINKING IN YOUR HOME

Here are some ideas for how to promote rational thinking in your home:

1. Encourage nonfiction reading. This will act as a nice counterbalance to the fiction your daughter may prefer.

In our house you can always find the *Oregonian* newspaper, *Wall Street Journal*, *Atlantic Monthly*, *Time*, and other periodicals.

2. Watch documentaries together. We are in the golden age of great documentary filmmaking. A lot of families binge watch TV series. Why not binge watch a few documentaries?

3. When your daughter is making a difficult decision, suggest she create a pros and cons list. This encourages thoughtful decision making.

4. Ask your daughter this question when you think she is making a mistake based on her own emotional state: Would you encourage your best friend to make this choice?

HELP HER UNDERSTAND SHE HAS VALUE

Where does an understanding of one's value come from? Ideally it comes from a lifetime of strong connections to loving parents. When parents love their children, protect them, invest in them, look them directly in the eyes on a regular basis and tell them they love them and hug them often, their children learn they are valuable.

The power of a parent's affirmation and love was brought home to me one day during a classroom discussion that had nothing to do with the day's planned subject matter. We were talking about parents grounding their children. One thing led to another, and soon many students were pouring out their hearts that their parents don't express love for them. It was nearly unbearable.

After class a teary-eyed student came up to me. I had talked many times before with this student about the struggles of living with her divorced, bipolar mother. I knew that what I was about to hear would not be good. And then she said, "Mr. Anderson, would you give me a hug? My father has never hugged me in my life." In all my years of teaching this was perhaps the most soul-crushing moment I had ever experienced. I ended that class with a big hug for that student. Every day for the rest of the semester when I greeted her at the door, she would ask for a hug. Sadly, my hugs weren't enough to fill the hole in her heart for her father's love. This young girl believed she was worthless, and it has played out in an eating disorder that has required two hospitalizations. While this young woman is on the road to recovery, I have always wondered what her life would have been like if her parents had given her the love and affirmation she needed. (As of this writing, this young woman has just graduated from a university and is now pursuing a master's in social work. She has not needed to go back into treatment for her eating disorder for more than three years.)

Jacquelyn:
Here are some ideas, based on what my parents did for me as a teen, for how you can help your daughter know her value.

- *Give her lots of hugs and kisses.* There is a tremendous amount of research out there about the power of physical touch. Part of being emotionally and physically healthy is not being starved for physical affection. To this day I sometimes like to hold my dad's hand, and he always gives it a squeeze. So, hug your daughter. In doing so, you reduce the chance that she will be hugging a random pubescent boy at school that day. Win-win.

- *Praise her for her efforts and hard work.* Too often we tie our worth to success or failure when in reality it is bound with fighting hard to be our best. The more you affirm that your daughter's efforts are appreciated and worthwhile, the more she will realize her intrinsic value. My dad writes the very best cards and letters. I have cherished those words my whole life for their love, encouragement, and pride in who I have become.

- *Tell her that you love her, that she is beautiful, that she is talented, that she is capable of great things.* As you might know, kind words from a stranger can turn around your whole day. Imagine the power of meaningful words from a loved and trusted parent! Use your words to show her that she has value. Be specific. Say these things often, really mean them—and then stand back and watch your daughter blossom.

Because my parents told me all of this on a regular basis, I always knew that they had my back and that they saw me as valuable. While I still made some mistakes, I cannot imagine what my life would be without their intentional building-me-up.

72

Of all the myths discussed in this book, your daughter may find this one about trusting her feelings the most challenging to her belief system. For many, many young women, their default setting is that emotions trump rational thinking. That is why it is so critical that in our role as parents we make every attempt to connect our daughters with rational thinking at every turn. Jacquelyn and I hope the suggestions and discussion questions in this chapter can go a long way toward guiding you in helping your daughter balance her emotions and thinking.

QUESTIONS FOR REFLECTION

1. What are some of the feelings you have had in life that you now know were false? Have you shared these with your daughter?
2. If your daughter has a boyfriend, how are you helping her keep the relationship in perspective? How might you help her to think about her relationship with logic and not just emotion?
3. In action and word, how are you teaching your daughter that she is valuable?

QUESTIONS FOR YOU AND YOUR DAUGHTER TO DISCUSS

1. How do you see yourself? Do you know you are valuable? Where does your value come from?
2. What is the difference between self-esteem and human value?
3. What are three things you would never do or allow others to do to you because you are valuable?

4. Do you have a friend or acquaintance who acts if she is not valuable? What behaviors do you see that show she doesn't feel valuable? Why is this belief dangerous for your friend?
5. Have you ever had a feeling that turned out to be wrong? How can you know in the future when a feeling isn't trustworthy?

LOOKING AHEAD TO THE NEXT CHAPTER

As a relationship unfolds and grows, the emotions are amplified. With each passing day the bond between two people grows. As emotions grab hold of a girl, they begin to become her most important reality. It is then that she will begin to believe dating myth #3: *I'm in love.*

Dating Myth #3

I'm in Love

When a girl is in the early stages of a relationship, what she feels is incredible. As adults our blood isn't as hot as it once was, but we can still remember what young love was like—no other feeling on earth! We wanted to spend every waking moment with our crush. Nothing has changed over the years.

When a teenage girl has a boyfriend, her focus, emotions, and life begin to center on that relationship. She talks about him. She dreams about him. She plans around him. But is what she feels for him love? In this chapter we will learn about why our daughters feel like it is. We will also learn about the biology of love so we can help them answer the question that consumes young lovers: Is this love?

WIRED TO LOVE

From the time girls are born, they are wired for emotional intimacy. In the last chapter we learned about the power of dopamine and oxytocin. These are like drugs in your daughter's system. When she is talking deeply with her close friends, dopamine and oxytocin are on the rise in her brain. Girls "get high" on emotional intimacy because it increases the amount of dopamine and oxytocin in their brains.

The default setting for all brains in the womb is female, and male and female brains are identical the first seven weeks in the womb. But something happens to boys in the eighth week that changes their brains forever. At this time male brains get a serious bath of testosterone. Cells in the areas of the brain that control communication begin to die off, and the parts of the brain that control aggression and sexual desire begin to grow more cells. The female brain goes on to develop in a different manner, with a far greater capacity for processing communication and emotion. From the womb, girls are just better at emotions. And these important differences between boys and girls will continue throughout life.[1]

I see these differences every day in my high school classroom. High school boys can be very clumsy in social interaction. They are awkward and inadvertently hurt other people's feelings. Some time ago a boy proclaimed loudly during a class discussion that "girls belong in the kitchen." The moment the words tumbled out of his mouth, the girls in the class were on him like a pack of wolves. He immediately started backtracking and trying to smooth it over, but to no avail. (Needless to say he didn't take any girl in that class to the prom!) This boy was unable to read the emotional context of the discussion and consequently said something offensive to the girls in the class. Girls rarely make this type of social miscue, but boys make it often. In fact, brain disorders that affect understanding social cues and emotional tones, such as autism spectrum disorders, are far more common in boys than girls.[2]

Girls are also better than boys at hearing emotional tones and responding to emotional cues.[3] As small children, girls are far more likely than boys to respond to the tone of a person's voice. Girls read facial expressions, vocal tones, and the unspoken language of emotions. In short, they have critical wiring for love that boys lack, which make them more adept at emotional intimacy. (We will read in later chapters how these emotional differences between boys and girls can create a number of problems.)

The average girl has the capacity to think about love and romance in ways that just don't occur to most boys. If you need convincing, look no further than romance novels. In 2010 romance novels sold a total of $1.4 billion in the United States. According to industry statistics, 82 percent of the readers of these novels were read by—you guessed it—women.[4]

A few years ago my wife and daughters read the Twilight series. In 2008 the four books in the series were numbers 1, 2, 3, and 4 on *USA Today*'s bestselling book list.[5] I decided to see what the buzz was about. Boy, was I disappointed. While my wife and daughters were enjoying each book in the series, all I could do was shake my head at yet another description of Edward Cullen's piercing gaze, strong arms, or beautiful lips. I finished the first book but decided someone might revoke my man card if I read any further. The series just didn't resonate with me. But for girls it really worked. It worked like *The Notebook*. It worked like *Titanic*. There is a reason romance novels sell, and that they call movies of this genre chick flicks. Girls, especially young girls, love romance and the idea of being in love.

Jacquelyn:

Just about every high school girl has to read *Romeo and Juliet*, and I was no exception. I sat in Mrs. Dowd's ninth-grade English class and, along with everyone else, struggled through the Shakespearean language to get to the core message underneath about the power of love. Romeo and Juliet's love was so strong that they were both willing to die for it. If you look at the play, or film, objectively, the plot borders on the ridiculous. I remember being flabbergasted when I realized that the entire love story took place over the course of just forty-eight hours. In just two days a thirteen-year-old girl and a fifteen-year-old boy meet, fall in love, and are willing to die for each other! This, folks, is the "greatest love story of our time." And it epitomizes your daughter's romanticized view of love.

Most girls want intimate connection *and* romance—to be swept off their feet and to be loved passionately. This is true for girls all over the world. Sometimes they convince themselves that what they are experiencing is love, when in reality they are just in love with the *idea* of being in love.

As parents we need to remember that our young daughters can feel romance very deeply. Their feelings may be immature and naive, but they are powerful nonetheless. To each of them, love is all about that butterfly feeling she gets in her stomach when she is with the one she "loves." The power of their feelings is often what makes them think that they are in love. What they don't realize is that their ideas about love are romanticized and uninformed. They have no understanding of what is happening in their brains.

WHAT'S HAPPENING IN HER BRAIN

Earlier we mentioned Helen Fisher's study of the three stages to relationships; the first stage being lust. Dr. Fisher posits that relationships have two other stages as well: attraction and attachment. Each stage happens in succession, and the previous stage must fade to allow the latter to emerge.[6] It is typically in the *attraction* phase of a relationship that a young girl thinks that what she feels for her boyfriend is love. During this phase, incredible changes occur in her brain circuitry. It's as if her brain and body are having a party.

If you were to look at your daughter's brain during the attraction phase of a relationship, you would see activity in the same part of the brain that controls such states as thirst, hunger, intoxication, and mania.[7] In fact, studies have found that the early stages of romance mimic the effects of the drug Ecstasy on the brain. Scientists speculate that a girl's preference for her boyfriend over nearly everything else may be a result of dopamine flooding her system.[8]

The attraction phase of romance is very much like addiction. During this phase, your daughter is becoming hooked on her boyfriend. You might say "she is crazy" about him, even intoxicated by him. One of the trademarks of drug addiction is that addicts will pursue the drug even when they are suffering serious consequences for their usage. The same is true when a girl is "addicted" to her boyfriend.

At this stage your daughter's craving for her boyfriend can be intense and the pursuit of the relationship can be all-consuming. What she is feeling is very strong. The emotional high, unlimited energy, sleeplessness, and downright craziness of attraction are difficult to put into words. Your daughter feels it right to her core, and it is a rush. But, as most adults know, this is not love.

I find it interesting that most girls, when encountering a boy for the first time, are good at sizing him up. During the first few minutes they assess his looks, personality, dress, and basic character. For example, my wife has an incredible capacity to see right through people in a way I never can. Many times over the years Tamara has said to me, "There is something wrong with that guy." She is right far more often than she is wrong. On one such occasion she was very suspect of a man known to our family. Several years later we learned that this man was a Peeping Tom. She knew something was wrong from the beginning because she has great instincts. I think girls use these instincts every day to keep themselves safe. In a world where boys are stronger and some are predatory, girls need to evaluate who a boy is in short order. A healthy dose of skepticism can keep a girl out of a dangerous situation.

However, during the attraction phase, a girl is much less likely to pick up on a boy's shortcomings. During this phase, when the female brain is turning up the areas of the brain that control love, it is also turning down the areas that control worry and critical thinking, making it much easier for the girl to let down her guard.[9] This is God's way of starting a spark between two people. If girls were hyperalert to boys' faults all the time, they would never be able to form relationships with the opposite gender. As she grows attached to her boyfriend, a girl is thinking less critically about him and beginning to view him through loving eyes. This is why a girl can go from not liking a boy at all to having quite an interest in him in just a few short days. Her affection cannot grow unless she sees the good in a person. But as they say, "not everything that glitters is gold."

This process of turning up love and turning down critical thinking can cause a girl to fall for the wrong guy. One time after class I was talking to a girl about her boyfriend. She was telling me how sweet he was and what a great boyfriend he was. They had been dating a few months, and she was definitely into him. The only problem, she said, was that he was in jail for assault. I tried to explain to her that someone in jail probably isn't the best choice for a boyfriend, but she wouldn't hear it. She continued to sing his praises. Her brain was helping her view her boyfriend in the best possible light. As she walked out of the room, she ended our conversation with a line I'll never forget: "He is a really great guy. He just has anger management issues." While her critical thinking and worry were turned down, I'm pretty sure her parents' were off the charts.

Jacquelyn:

Expressing your concerns about your daughter's significant other can be the most stressful and tricky conversation you may ever have with her. Although I never slammed my bedroom door in my parents' faces, there were times when I felt angry and frustrated about something they said or did. So, when you have these kinds of conversations, remember to try to be cool as a cucumber. "Freaking out" is the number one thing that parents do that kids can't handle. When you get intense and emotional, it serves only to escalate the situation.

In addition, save these talks until you can have them when your daughter is a captive audience. My mom has many times blindsided me with some truth spoken in love: in the car, at lunch, around the house. Remind your daughter that you love her and want only the best for her; express your concerns in a calm way, and then try to leave it at that. Teenagers don't want to be told the same thing over and over again, and your doing so will only drive a wedge in your relationship.

In the end, your daughter will do what she wants to do—she may even choose to stay with a boy you don't like. Hopefully, she will listen to your counsel and hightail it out of there. If she makes the wise choice, then that is great! If she doesn't, freaking out about it will only further separate her from you and push her closer to her boyfriend.

THE FALLOUT OF BELIEVING THIS MYTH: STUPID SACRIFICES

When a teen girl believes she is in love, it can lead her to make some unwise and even dangerous choices.

Years ago when I was teaching in a small-town high school, I had a student who was making stupid sacrifices. Because she thought she was in love, she had given up much of her life to her boyfriend. Before they began dating, this girl had many friends. She was active in athletics and had terrific grades. But that all changed when she got into a serious relationship. Little by little she gave over parts of her life to her boyfriend. She was sacrificing who she was and what she did in order to spend more time with him. Her grades began to falter. She quit playing sports. She never spent any time with her friends. In fact, every day while her boyfriend was at basketball practice, she would sit in the corner of the gym and wait for him to finish. Things progressed from bad to worse.

I was one of her boyfriend's basketball coaches, and one day before practice I noticed that the players on the team were gathered by the gym doors, looking out into the parking lot. They were gesturing and laughing, so I decided to see what was up. I saw them pointing to a car in the parking lot whose sole occupant, this girl's boyfriend, seemed to be having a really good time. I mean a *really* good time. He appeared to be alone, but it soon became clear he was not. Though you could not see my student, she was performing oral sex on him. At that moment the head coach walked up to me and saw what was going on. He ran out to the parking lot and pounded on the car window. The girl popped up. She should have been humiliated, but she didn't seem to care. A few minutes later the boy came into the gym and started practice. She walked in, right on his heels, and sat in the corner to watch him, just like she did every day.

Sadly, this girl had sacrificed her interests, her self-worth, and her dignity to this guy. Granted, this example is extreme, but girls who are willing to make stupid sacrifices for their boyfriends in less critical areas are on their way to making stupid sacrifices that may haunt them the rest of their lives.

As parents we need to teach our daughters to be able to identify stupid sacrifices. A girl needs to know that if she will someday say, "I can't believe I did that for him," then what she is about to do is a stupid sacrifice. Every action *she is about to make* and every request he makes *of her* should be seen through this lens.

You may be thinking, *If her judgment has been suspended because she is head over heels, how can a girl know what she will regret later?* I'm not sure I have an answer for that question. But I do know this: as parents we have to try and try and try to get our daughters to think with the long view in mind, not just the here and now. So be proactive. Talk to your daughter about what a stupid sacrifice is long before she begins dating. Give her an idea of what real love looks like. When a girl is in the early attachment stage of a relationship, she might not have a good reference point for what real love looks like. It is your job to help her understand this. And this may be the best thing you can do to help her avoid making stupid sacrifices.

> *Jacquelyn:*
>
> If my parents had had a conversation like this with me when I was young, I think it would have helped for them to give me examples of what kinds of things are stupid sacrifices. Maybe try asking your daughter about some of the relationships she sees kids involved in at her school and some of the sacrifices she sees girls making for their boyfriends. Affirm her thoughts when she recognizes stupid sacrifices. In addition, help her come up with examples of what sacrifice for real love looks like. One thing that helped me grasp this concept was watching the healthy and loving marriage my parents shared. They both sacrificed for each other and also for our family.

WHAT IS REAL LOVE?

If you've ever been to a wedding, you've probably heard this well-known and beautiful description of what love is. It comes from the New Testament and was written over 1,950 years ago. Yet it is as true today as it was then:

Love never gives up.

Love cares more for others than for self.

Love doesn't want what it doesn't have.

Love doesn't strut,

Doesn't have a swelled head,

Doesn't force itself on others,

Isn't always "me first,"

Doesn't fly off the handle,

Doesn't keep score of the sins of others,

Doesn't revel when others grovel,

Takes pleasure in the flowering of truth,

Puts up with anything, …

Love never dies.[10]

Any discussion about what real love is should probably start with this wisdom. Your daughter needs to understand that real love should mirror this teaching. She also needs to realize that real love takes time to grow and is sacrificial.

REAL LOVE TAKES TIME TO DEVELOP

Real love takes time to grow. One study shows that when a girl is in the third stage of a relationship, attachment, her brain is much different from when it is in the lust and attraction stages. In this study, scientists scanned the brains of couples who had on average been in the relationship 2.3 years and who had stated that they were "in love." Scans revealed that the most active part of their brains was the area that controls mutual bonding—not the part that controls passionate love.[11] Researchers believe a different part of the brain may be at work in the attachment phase than during the lust and attraction phases. (Maybe this network is the deep roots of love?) In most cases when a young girl believes she is in love, the relationship is far too new for her to be in love and has not developed and matured into the attachment phase. It is very important that young girls understand that real love develops slowly.

REAL LOVE IS SACRIFICIAL

As adults we view the quality of love by what people are willing to sacrifice for one another. Sacrifice is at the heart of real love. What are we willing to give up for the other person? Are we willing to sacrifice our desires and needs?

Tamara and I have been married for twenty-seven years. Every day is about sacrifice. I cannot live for myself each day because that would be selfish. Nor can she live for herself each day. We must live for each other. That is how a marriage grows, matures, and lasts. Because I love my wife, I've chosen to sacrifice some of my aspirations to make her dreams possible. Case in point: For quite a while I aspired to be a high school basketball coach in the inner city. When I began my teaching career at an urban Portland school, I thought I was going to be the next White Shadow. (You might need to Google that one if you are not a man over the age of forty-five.) This was my dream, but the hours are grueling, the emotional investment is high, and the stress can be toxic. As I embarked on my coaching career, it became obvious that if I were to go down that path, it would make my wife miserable and endanger our marriage.

I had to give up coaching and all that it entailed. The hours of time away from the family. The stress of wins and losses. The meetings, awards, practices, games, and tournaments, which required minute attention to every detail. There was no way our relationship could have flourished while I was a coach. To help her be happy, I had to give up something. My wife has always done the same for me. This is what love is all about.

When teenage girls begin to fall in love, they typically ask themselves some serious questions. Should I have sex with my boyfriend? Should I spend less time with my friends and more time with him? Should I tell my parents about him? (Sorry, parents. In a world where teens "hang out" and communicate via social media more than they date, your daughter may very well have love feelings for a boy you have never met.) As these girls become young women, they also ask things such as: Should I go to college where he is going? Should I move to be closer to him? Should we live together? Should we get married?

Many of these questions have life-changing implications. Let's explore some ideas for helping your daughter answer the question, is this love? A girl's answers may determine the course of her life, as the consequences of some choices cannot be undone.

PREPARING YOUR DAUGHTER FOR FUTURE HAPPINESS

It is our job as parents to help our daughters make smart choices about whom to date and to teach them how to identify the difference between the thrill of attraction and the stability of attachment. The ideal time for discussing these issues is before your daughter even begins dating, but even if it is too late for that, these conversations are worth having. Here are some ideas to get you started.

GUIDE HER IN BEING SMART ABOUT WHOM SHE DATES

Talk with your daughter about what the make-or-break character traits in a man are so that she can accurately assess potential boyfriends—and eventually a potential spouse. I believe both Mom and Dad will have distinct ideas in this area; so input from both parents will be invaluable. This awareness will go a long ways in ensuring that your daughter doesn't have a broken picker—that she won't fall into the trap of dating boys who are not good for her.

My wife and I have tried to teach our daughters that in order for a boy to be worthy of their interest, he must have certain character traits. We've taught them that they have value—they are the *imago Dei*—and that they need to choose boys who mirror that value. Even as I was trying to stop Jackie from dating, it was my hope that when she did start to date she would have strong standards for a boy. In the years since, I have asked my daughters what they are looking for in a boy and to write up a list. Tamara and I have been open with our children about the type of person we'd like them to be with. There is, of course, no guarantee that our kids will take our advice into account. But even so, I think that encouraging teens to think about the qualities they are looking for in a date and to write down their answers will also help them think more logically about the people they get involved with romantically.

Jacquelyn:

While my parents and I didn't have this conversation when I was in high school, we have had it often in the years since. They usually ask me what I am looking for in a guy I want to date and what I am looking for in a husband—and then make some of their own suggestions. You might prime the pump by asking your daughter questions such as: What qualities does your dream guy have? Is he a Christian? What would you like his family structure to look like? How does he treat his family? Would you be happy if he had been in lots of relationships before? What are the three most important personality traits that you think he needs to have? What kinds of school activities do you want him to be involved in? Does he get good grades? Then, encourage her to measure every potential suitor by her list. This will help her suss out what she is looking for. When I am interested in a guy, my parents ask me these same sets of questions to help make sure that the choice I am making is a smart one.

But it's not enough to have a list of qualities. As our daughters date, they need to learn to look for "the moments"—those instances when the character of the boy they are dating is tested and revealed. For my oldest sister this same type of moment came early in her relationship with her future husband. While they were driving down the freeway during a terrible ice storm, a car in front of them lost control and crashed. In that moment her boyfriend was unfazed. In that moment he acted with strength and unflappability and his character confirmed this was a fella for her. They have been married for thirty-four years.

If the boy's character fails the test, let your daughter know she needs to have the insight and strength to move on. Our daughters need to hear us tell them over and over not to spend one more minute, emotion, or tear on a boy who demonstrates that he is not worthy of their love. For nearly forty years L'Oréal's commercial tagline was "Because I'm worth it." Our daughters need to live like they are in a L'Oréal commercial.

Which leads me to the question, What do you do when your daughter has interest in someone you believe isn't good for her? How do you guide her to date smart then? Like so many dilemmas in parenting, there is no one-size-fits-all answer. However, unless she has brought home a boy who is an immediate and serious threat to her, you may need to let the situation play out a bit. Be wary of taking a hard-line approach. To a certain degree your daughter cannot help what she is feeling. You may not be happy with her choice, but the more you push against her, the more she may lean into the boyfriend. Instead, I recommend that you closely monitor the relationship and be ready to take drastic action if it is needed.

TEACH HER ABOUT THE THREE STAGES OF A RELATIONSHIP

You and your daughter should be conversant with the terms *lust*, *attraction*, and *attachment*. If she has never heard these words and doesn't know how the three stages differ from one another, how can she hope to be discerning about what she really feels for her boyfriend?

As parents we need to remember that if a girl has been in a relationship for just a few months, her feelings for her boyfriend are likely the strongest emotions she has ever felt in her life. If she does not know the difference between *attraction* and *attachment*, she is likely to begin making choices and actions based on the idea that she is in love. The more she understands the difference between attraction and attachment, the smarter she will be in her relationship choices.

Help her understand what real love is, and that sacrifice (not stupid sacrifice) is very much the heart of love. If your daughter is in a relationship, she should ask herself a few questions: Does he open doors for me? Does he ask me my preference on dates? Is he willing to make time for me even though he may have a busy schedule? Does he often put my needs ahead of his own? These are all ways in which a teen boy can demonstrate a willingness to be sacrificial. From the earliest stages of a relationship, our daughters need to know that if a boy is not sacrificial toward her, then he is not worthy of her. Too many young girls stick around with jerky, selfish boys because they do not understand that attraction and attachment are different.

I also encourage you to tell your daughter the story of how your marriage relationship unfolded. As early as her middle school years, take an opportunity to tell her about how you moved from attraction to attachment. Let her know how long you were in the relationship before you knew it was the deep love of attachment.

TEACH HER TO ASK HERSELF, "IS THIS SOMETHING I WILL REGRET LATER?"

Consider discussing the following list of stupid sacrifices with your daughter, encouraging her to think about the impact of these choices and how she might feel about their consequences, particularly if the relationship ends.

1. You ditch your friends mid-movie so you can call and talk with your boyfriend.

2. You stay home on a Friday night just in case your boyfriend gets done early from his other activity and wants to hang out.

3. You skip a trip going anywhere on this planet so you can spend time with your boyfriend.

4. You let your grades suffer so you can talk, chat, and text with your boyfriend more.

5. You quit any sport, play, job, musical, or other activity you enjoy to spend more time with your boyfriend.

6. You skip a class in school to hang out with your boyfriend. (This is doubly stupid sacrifice. You are getting stupider by not going to class.)

7. You spend less time with your best friends to spend more time with your boyfriend.

8. You lie to your parents about where you are going so you can see your boyfriend.

9. You do things sexually that you think are wrong and inconsistent with who you are and who you want to be.

ENCOURAGE HER TO ESTABLISH TIME AND COMMUNICATION BOUNDARIES

As parents we need to help our daughters maintain limits and boundaries while they are young. All too often I encounter parents who are checked out when it comes to their daughter's relationship with her boyfriend. The girl is venturing without mature direction and acting on her own instincts and going places emotionally and physically that are not good for her, yet the parents stand idly by. It is our job as parents to help our daughters understand where safe and healthy limits are when it comes to relationships.

Jacquelyn:

Here are some suggestions that I think would have helped guide and protect me when I was a teenage girl. Your daughter is probably not going to like some of these, but I can guarantee you that she will thank you for them later.

- Help your daughter practice the one-to-one ratio for boyfriend and friends. If she spends Saturday with her boyfriend, make sure she spends Sunday with her girlfriends. It is important that her circle of friends remains intact for many reasons.
- Do not allow her to be on the computer or accessing the Internet on her smartphone or iPad behind a closed door. Definitely do not allow her to have a cell phone in her room when it's time for her to be in bed. At the very least you can help ensure your daughter a good night's sleep uninterrupted by the buzzing of the phone. My parents did a really great job of this, and I think that I'm a better person for it. This boundary was true of talking to girlfriends as well.
- Try your hardest to make sure your daughter is engaged in a variety of activities that don't involve

her boyfriend. Encourage her to join a club, sport, or activity that interests her and helps her create other sources of connection and relationship. My dad was especially supportive of me creating a community of wonderful women who surround me still to this day.

- Don't let your daughter ever spend unsupervised time alone with her significant other. Need I say more?

- Help your daughter maintain separation from her family life. She needs to realize that unless she is married to him, her boyfriend is not part of your family. Don't take him on family vacations, don't have him over for the holidays, and definitely don't let him live with you.

  If your daughter wants to break up with her boyfriend, she needs to make the break as clean and quick as possible. If you have involved him in your family, this makes it much more difficult for her to do this. He needs to know that he is on the outside of your family and that your daughter is on the inside.

People who have balance in their lives recognize that a dating or marriage relationship is just one facet of their identity. While my marriage is a top priority for me, it does not define who I am. Nor should a relationship define your daughter. A dating relationship should be one part of a rich and full life. A healthy relationship has room for friends, family, sports, hobbies, passions, and more. A healthy dating relationship is one in which time apart is as important as time together; it is one in which the feeling of love is balanced against the understanding of what real love is. If we can help our daughters make this distinction, they will be far more likely to date smart.

QUESTIONS FOR REFLECTION

1. How have you communicated to your daughter what the mature love of attachment is?
2. In what ways do you believe your daughter's expectations in a dating relationship have been influenced by what she has seen in movies and on television?
3. Have you ever committed stupid sacrifices? Why did you do that? Can you share any of these experiences with your daughter?
4. Have you ever mistaken the idea of being in love with actually being in love? If so, how can you communicate that to your daughter?

QUESTIONS FOR YOU AND YOUR DAUGHTER TO DISCUSS

1. Have you ever misjudged a boy? In what ways were you wrong about him? How did your emotions cloud your judgment?
2. Do you think you or any of your friends have ever gone past the attraction phase to the attachment phase? If so, how long did it last? Is the relationship still happening? How can you tell it is attachment and not just attraction?

3. When do you believe you should tell a boy that you love him?

4. How important are the opinions of your close friends and family when judging the character of your boyfriend? What would you do if everyone you were close to did not approve of your choice in a boy?

5. Are any of your friends or acquaintances making stupid sacrifices? What does that look like, and how do you think it impacts their lives?

LOOKING AHEAD TO THE NEXT CHAPTER

As girls begin to experience what they believe is love, they want to express their emotions with greater intimacy and closeness. The natural path love follows leads many girls to sexual intimacy. As a girl begins a sexual relationship, dating myth #4 will emerge: *Sex will enhance my relationship.*

Dating Myth #4

Sex Will Enhance My Relationship

Have you seen the Subaru commercial in which the father lovingly explains to his five-year-old daughter about adjusting the mirrors, staying off the freeway, and not texting and then hands over the car keys for her to pull out of the driveway? It is only when she begins to back the car out that we see the girl is all grown up and that he just *sees* a five-year-old.

I have to confess that my life is one big Subaru commercial. As my daughters have grown up, I'm not sure I've grown up with them. I think it may be true for many dads out there. In our mind's eye our daughters will always be "Daddy's little girl." Because of this we can have a hard time wrapping our heads around their emerging sexuality. I shared earlier that as my daughters grew up, I came to see the boys in their lives as the enemies. I believed it was my job to protect my daughters from the pubescent, testosterone-crazed boys who have only one thing on their minds. (I wish that last sentence was an exaggeration, but I swear I mean every single word of it.) I don't believe there is anything more difficult for the average man than to see his daughter begin to take an interest in sex and boys. As a result, we dads are going to need help from the moms in this world to get through this period of our daughters' lives.

After a girl reaches puberty, she may feel as if everything in her entire world points toward having sex. It is the milestone by which many mark their lives. Throughout middle school and beyond, sex is an undercurrent in nearly everything people do and say. For young people it hangs in the air like the smell of fresh-baked cookies, warm and delicious. Boys think about it all the time. Girls talk about it. As our daughters grow into young adults, sex permeates so many of their conversations and interactions that it feels as though it is just part of the pattern of their lives.

Jacquelyn:

This is true, even for Christian girls. Because sex was a taboo topic, it made it even more interesting for my friends and me to think about and talk about.

The message I got from my parents about sex was basically "Don't do it." This was good advice, but I don't think it went far enough. Most of the girls I knew in high school were also in church youth groups. Only a few of them remained virgins until their weddings. While your daughter may have lots of Christian friends or be actively involved in church, this does not mean that her dating relationship will take a different path from her non-Christian friends'.

What I wish my parents had told me was the *why*. Yes, don't do it, but why not? Not just what the Bible says about it, but what kind of long-term consequences can sex have on a girl's emotional and spiritual health? Sex leaves teenage girls feeling used and broken. Why doesn't anybody tell girls that?

Adolescence is such a weird time, especially for a girl. Our bodies and brains are, in many ways, ready to get married, have sex, and have babies. In Bible times, I would have been married with two kids by the time I graduated from high school. Biologically and culturally, sex is a teenage experience.

For most teenage girls the expected path of a dating relationship leads to sex. I'd like to think this is not true in the Christian community, but research tells a different story. Several studies have shown that fully 80 percent of evangelical Christians aged eighteen to twenty-nine have already had sex.[1] Bear in mind that even if your daughter doesn't assume that sex will enhance her relationship, she is likely surrounded by girls who do, and she is being bombarded by this message. Given this reality, every parent must be the counterbalance to a culture that tells teenage girls that premarital sex is a normal part of any dating relationship.

At this point you might be thinking, *But I don't want to talk to my daughter about sex!* It might surprise you, but your daughter probably doesn't want to talk to you about sex either. Such conversations can feel awkward, weird, uncomfortable. But if you want your daughter to be accurately informed, you need to be sure she gets her information about sex from you first, rather than from her friends.

Jacquelyn:

I remember my grade school best friend was considered the "expert" on sex on the playground. We all sat inside the wooden fort while she enlightened us with her "vast understanding" of this forbidden topic. Needless to say, everything she said was inaccurate. She had to whisper because she didn't want the duty teacher to hear, but in hushed tones she told us that women got pregnant through their belly buttons. See what I mean?

With the goal of helping you understand what is happening with your daughter, we'll talk frankly in this chapter about why people want to have sex and we'll blow up the myth that says sex enhances a young girl's relationship.

WHY GIRLS WANT TO HAVE SEX

Scientists understand much of the biology of female sexual desire, but the psychology of sexual desire is still a bit of a mystery. Female sexuality is enormously complex, and a girl's motives for sex are often complicated and overlapping. Fortunately, there are some well-understood insights into female sexual desire, and they point to some safe assumptions we can make about why girls want to have sex.

IT FEELS GOOD

Sex feels good. That much is obvious. What may not be obvious is why it feels so good. The answer is dopamine. When people are enjoying the skin-to-skin contact of physical touch, dopamine is the reward. If a little touching delivers a little dopamine, then a lot of touching will deliver even more. One important research finding is that new experiences release even more dopamine than things we have already encountered.[2] This explains why the first time you do something—say bungee jumping—it feels terrific but the returns diminish the more you do it. Early-stage physical intimacy is no different.

You might remember a time when young people spoke daringly of "getting to first base" or "getting to second base." Over time first base isn't good enough, or second, or third. Like all people, your daughter is hardwired to need dopamine, and few things in life deliver more dopamine than sex. Because physical intimacy and foreplay feel good, she wants to hit a "home run."

The desire for sex is healthy, normal, and needed. I think some parents lose sight of this. God created sex to be enjoyable so that we would want to have it. We are made different from animals, which do everything by instinct. For example, the migratory patterns of animals cannot be altered. A wildebeest on the plains of the Serengeti has to migrate. It cannot think, *I don't feel like migrating this year.* It is the animal's instinct to migrate. But we humans are much more complex and extraordinary than animals. If we were like animals and driven solely by instinct, the urge to have sex would overtake us, similar to the wildebeest's need to migrate. The results would not be pretty. It would be sex anywhere, anytime, with anyone. I realize that it seems as if some people actually operate this way. However, because we are created in the image of God, with free will, we have the ability to choose whether we have sex. God made sex physically pleasurable so that we would choose it. It is part of God's plan for lifetime partnership.

However, if a girl is having sex solely for the physical pleasure it brings, then she is not experiencing sex in the way she is best designed to enjoy it. One of the things that separates boys from girls is the degree to which girls put their emotional selves into sexual intimacy, which brings us to the second reason girls want to have sex.

SHE WANTS TO EXPERIENCE THE FULL CLOSENESS OF SEXUAL INTIMACY

Girls also want to have sex because of the emotions they are feeling. In an emotionally healthy girl, the desire to have sex is grounded in emotional connection. As her relationship grows, she feels close to her boyfriend and begins to desire the physical intimacy that is complementary to her feelings. Because she is in a close relationship, her level of trust increases and she wants to experience the full closeness of sexual intimacy. Sex cements two people together.

Jacquelyn:
Just to be clear, teen girls *dream* that sex will make them feel closer to their boyfriend, but during high school, I didn't know a single girl who was having sex and getting this full, intimate, close experience. It just isn't a part of the teenage sexual experience. Teens aren't capable of the love or connectedness required to feel that kind of intimacy. Of all the teen girls I knew who were having sex, I would be hard

pressed to think of any who were completely connected or fulfilled by their experiences.

While the two reasons we've covered are healthy, there are a few unhealthy reasons girls want to have sex.

SHE FEELS PRESSURED

Over the years I've come to realize that girls are under a great deal of pressure to have sex. I see it in the comments of both boys and girls in class discussions. As relationships with young people unfold, the *expectation* of sex commonly begins to drive the relationship. Girls often say that they are afraid their boyfriends will break up with them if they don't have sex. For too many girls this fear is deep seated and pervasive.

Jacquelyn:
When I was a teen, this pressure didn't come just from boys; sometimes it came from other girls. Sometimes it simply trickled down from the culture at large. The message my friends and I received was that there was a timeline for relationships and that at a certain point the logical step was sex.

SHE FEELS LACKING IN SOMETHING AND THINKS SEX IS THE ANSWER

I've seen over and over that the most vulnerable, weak, and wounded girls are the ones likely to be involved in unhealthy, sexually active relationships. Maybe they feel ugly. Maybe they feel lonely. Maybe their parents have wounded them. Whatever the reason, some girls look to sex to get the love, acceptance, and validation they feel they lack.

When I was younger, I went dancing with a friend at the Portland Club Plaza (cue '80s synth-pop dance track now). Soon after my friend entered the club, he would spend a few minutes looking over the girls on the dance floor. Then he would approach one of them and ask her to dance. He nearly always ended up making out with her and oftentimes went home with her. I asked him once how he did it, and he said he didn't know.

I've learned over the years that many boys have radars for weak and needy girls. It is a truly awful gift. Girls need to understand that in general boys are willing to sleep with as many girls as they can. (We'll talk more about this in the next section.)

SHE BELIEVES HAVING SEX WILL EMPOWER HER

A pervasive belief in our culture is harming young women tremendously; its message says that by having sex you are demonstrating your own empowerment and sexual freedom. As such, you would expect few regrets on the part of young women in sexual relationships. However, quite the opposite is true. Particularly when it comes to uncommitted sex. Though we will address "hookup sex" extensively in chapter 6, it is worth noting here that several studies indicate that up to three-fourths of young women have feelings of regret from uncommitted sex.[3] That being the case, how can sex be empowering and freeing?

Jacquelyn:

You might be thinking, *My daughter doesn't think that!* I'm here to say that the pervasive message she is hearing is that sex will empower her. "Sex is cool; sex is great; have it whenever you want with whomever you want." This message is all around her! While girls should not feel shame for having sexual desire—it is a part of who God made us to be—the idea that sex will make a teenage girl feel empowered is a total lie. When my friends talk about losing their virginity in high school, which some of your daughter's friends will do, they all have a very powerless and awful story to tell. In contrast, when my friends who waited to have sex talk about their first experience, the story is one of joy, love, and freedom within the bounds of a committed relationship that was able to handle that kind of connection.

It is important that our daughters understand the ways in which a boy's desire for sex differs from theirs so they won't get caught up in thinking that sex will strengthen their relationship.

HOW BOYS ARE DIFFERENT WHEN IT COMES TO SEX
HIS DESIRE IS TRIGGERED VISUALLY; HERS IS TRIGGERED EMOTIONALLY

For boys of any age, the desire for sex is a visual—not an emotional—thing. It is well known that the male brain on average is 9 percent larger than the female brain.[4] (The old joke is that the 9 percent must be dedicated to looking at girls!) The scientific evidence for this is overwhelming: when a male sees naked girls, an MRI shows his brain lighting up like a Christmas tree. This isn't the case in females, who are less affected by visual imagery.[5]

Cross-cultural studies show that boys are far more interested in a girl's appearance when looking for a long-term partner than in other factors. Girls are exactly the opposite. Research submits that they value social status and personality much more than appearance.[6] To put it simply, boys experience sexual desire through a visual filter; girls through an emotional filter. This is why it is common to see an attractive girl date a less attractive boy, but not the other way around. (I'm living proof of this phenomenon: I definitely married up.) Girls "date down" because they take the whole boy into consideration—personality, charisma, money, status, and looks. Why are boys much less willing to date down? Because much of a boy's love preference is driven by visual information.

I often tell my students that there are two reasons boys will have sex. The first is because a girl is naked. Her nakedness (or just the potential for nakedness!) triggers the desire for sex. And to be honest it doesn't matter much who the girl is. Research shows that when looking for a hookup, boys are willing to get with girls who are less athletic, funny, educated, loyal, stable, and of nearly any age.[7] The second reason is an available girl. For many boys, if a girl is naked *and* available (and if she will agree to it), then they will have sex with her. It is that simple.

Under the category of "hard to believe" is an experiment conducted in 1978 and again in 1989. In this experiment researchers took an attractive girl on a college campus and had her approach a college boy, saying, "I have been noticing you around campus. I find you to be very attractive." Then she would ask either, "Would you go out with me tonight?"; "Would you come over to my apartment tonight?"; or "Would you go to bed with me tonight?" Among the boys in the experiment 75 percent agreed to have sex with the girl. Of course the study would never allow the boy to sleep with the girl. (There were likely many disappointed boys in this study!) When this experiment was reversed with an attractive boy asking girls the same three questions, the results were different.[8] No girls agreed to have sex with the boy.

The issue of casual sex with a stranger was addressed again in a 2011 study using questionnaires rather than the face-to-face experiment done in 1989. The 2011 study had similar data results for anonymous sex requests.[9] Though less definitive in its findings than the classic study, one thing is clear: boys are far more likely to engage in opportunistic sex with a stranger than will girls.

You can see the opportunistic nature of male sexual desire in one study that indicates men are thirteen times more likely to want to participate in group sex than women.[10] In another study college boys and girls were asked, "How many sexual partners would you like over your lifetime if you were not stopped by law or disease?" The average number for the girl respondents was 2.7. For the boys it was 64.[11] Sixty-four! In short, some boys will hit anything with a pulse. I once found a wallet on the ground in my classroom. It belonged to a freshman boy and contained exactly two items: a school identification card and a condom. My mother used to call this "magical thinking." Despite the fantastical nature of his thoughts, this boy didn't care one bit about who he might sleep with. He just wanted to make sure he had a condom.

For a boy, sex and emotions are mostly separate from each other. If your daughter does not understand this fact, she is liable to misunderstand the male desire for sex. She will believe it is special and based on his feelings for her, when in fact it may be something else altogether.

FOR HIM, SEX IS THE REASON FOR THE RELATIONSHIP; FOR HER, THE RELATIONSHIP IS THE REASON FOR SEX

If having sex is a like a resort destination, then boys get there by train. The route is direct and with as few stops as possible. The trip is straightforward and speedy, and the train doesn't get off the tracks until it arrives at the station. For boys, the destination is more important than the journey.

In dating myth #2 we talked about the research that indicates that when a boy meets a girl for the first time, he will routinely present himself as funnier, more charming, and smarter than he actually is. What does this research really mean? It means that some boys, particularly younger boys, will lie to have sex with girls. This may be a cynical view of boys, but I can tell you it is true.

Granted, some boys may not be out-and-out lying, but their behavior and attention to a girl is very much kindled by an interest in sex. Think of it as a white lie. These boys *give* relational intimacy to *get* sex. All boys understand this is the deal.

In most cases girls control how quickly a boy will travel to the destination. Boys know that if they want to get there faster, they need to have their girlfriend feeling positive about the status of the relationship. In a mature, married man this looks like tending and caring for a wife; in an immature, young man this looks a great deal like inauthenticity and feigned interest—whatever it takes to get to the destination.

If sex is a destination, then girls travel by tour bus. They're not in a big hurry. Much of their enjoyment is what they experience along the way. The experiences, sights, sounds, and the trip are what make arriving at the destination so enjoyable. For most girls the journey matters, not just the arrival point. Unlike boys, girls travel the route to intimacy in a less direct manner. For girls who are emotionally healthy, the relationship is the reason for sex. They desire a relationship that helps them enjoy the destination once they arrive, and feelings of love, intimacy, and closeness are the heart of the journey.

Because boys and girls prefer to arrive at the destination in different ways, it can create problems. When a girl feels love and bonding with her boyfriend, it increases her desire for sex. For emotionally healthy girls, the relational journey must be enjoyable in order for sex to be emotionally and physically rewarding. Herein lies the problem. As we've seen, boys don't need the feelings of love to have sex. In most cases, once a boy has had sex with a girl, he will want sex again and again. He will want the direct route to sex each and every time; he doesn't need a journey, and he is always packed and ready to go!

Here's why. When a male has sex, his body produces a hormone called vasopressin. This hormone has quite an impact. Scientists believe it makes boys more focused, aggressive, and energetic.[12] It would be easy to translate the words *focused, aggressive,* and *energetic* into another word: *horny.* A boy's natural wiring to have lots of sex is magnified once he is having sex. Sex produces vasopressin, which makes boys hornier, which makes them have more sex, which produces more vasopressin, and so on. This problem is magnified by the fact that young men don't have the brain maturation to make good, healthy choices about expressing their sexual desires. Like a snowball rolling down a hill, once it's rolling, a boy's sex drive can be unstoppable.

SHORT DETOUR: A CAUTIONARY TALE FOR PARENTS

When you drive through a tunnel, everything is dark and hard to see except the light at the end of the tunnel. For boys, sex creates the ultimate case of tunnel vision. Nothing else matters. All a boy can see is the possibility of sex and he is blind to nearly everything else, and in some cases this may include the safety and security of your daughter. Here's a hard-to-read story that parents need to read and accept as the reality of the world in which their daughters are living.

My first sexual experience definitely changed the way I think about sex. During the fall of my freshman year of high school, my older brother had some friends from his football team stay the night. Two boys were on the couch, my brother was asleep in a chair, and I was asleep on the floor—as was D, a friend of my brother's whom I'd just met. While I was sleeping, D took my hand and put it on his genitals. I woke up, confused, in the darkness, because he was moving my hand up and down. When he noticed I'd woken up, he put his body on top of mine and covered my mouth with his free hand. I had only been kissed one time before this (by my middle school boyfriend) and didn't understand fully what was happening. I said "No, no, stop" several times through his hand.

When this episode was over, I left the basement and went to my bedroom upstairs, only to have him come again to my room. Even the next morning, I didn't understand why I hadn't screamed. If I'd screamed loud enough, my parents would have heard me. One thought was overriding all others as I looked at the dark figure in my doorway, and as he walked to my bed, as he climbed on top of me. My brother had told me earlier that day how this guy "might not be the biggest on the team, but he's definitely the strongest."

It was the first time I'd felt this type of gender difference. Most of the time, guys don't use this strength to do anything malicious to girls. Sometimes they aren't aware of what they're doing. And sometimes they use their physical strength to make something happen: to put you in a situation you don't want to be in, to keep you in that situation, and to make you feel like it'd be fruitless (or dangerous) to try to escape from it.

When he shoved his tongue past my clenched jaw, my brain was thinking how heavy he felt on top of me: I'd never felt this type of weight before. I couldn't move. "No, no, stop." My eyes were closed the whole time he was trying to rape me. When I started crying, something finally clicked with him and he got off me and left. My words hadn't registered with him, but my tears had.

I haven't spoken to him since that night.

In this searing account of attempted rape, notice how sex and emotions were not connected for the boy. The emotional context for this assault was fear, confusion, and coercion. This was what the girl was feeling. But the boy was sexually aroused despite what was emotionally ugly. As parents we need to understand this reality and protect our daughters from getting into situations where they might be sexually assaulted—whether from a stranger, acquaintance, or boyfriend.

When I first heard this story, I was appalled that these parents had sanctioned a coed sleepover. What were they thinking? Unfortunately coed sleepovers like this are common. On several occasions I told my own children they could not go to coed sleepovers with kids from church or from their Christian school. It is as if parents have forgotten what it was like to be young. I have a difficult time imagining when a coed sleepover would *ever* be a good idea, no matter where or with whom.

The truth is, sexual assault by a stranger is far less common than sexual assault by a friend or an acquaintance. According to the US Department of Justice, a girl under the age of twenty-four who has been sexually assaulted will know her attacker over 75 percent of the time. For a girl sexually assaulted between the ages of twelve to seventeen, 90 percent of those assaults will be committed by someone she knows.[13]

Another aspect of the story that I find disturbing is that this girl did not tell anyone about what had happened to her until years later. She didn't feel safe enough to tell her parents and never got the support she needed to process what had happened. On top of that, the boy was never confronted or punished. I only hope he never did those things again to another girl.

I have a question for you: *If something like this happened to your daughter, would she tell you?* I am deadly serious. Does your daughter feel safe enough to tell you of a sexual assault? Are you approachable? Are you available? Would you be able to suspend judgment if this happened to your daughter? Let this disturbing fact sink in: *the majority of sexual assaults in America go unreported.* In a most troubling statistic, the Department of Justice said that in 2010 only 27 percent of all sexual assaults and rapes were reported.[14] You must be certain your daughter will tell you if she is ever sexually assaulted.

"WHAT HAPPENED TO HIM? HE USED TO BE SO NICE"

Here is where we get to the heart of this myth. When a girl is invested emotionally in a dating relationship and is sexually active, initially sex may seem as though it is making the relationship better. She is getting the oxytocin and dopamine she needs from the physical intimacy, so she feels loved and cherished. He's happy because he's having lots of sex. Both of them seem to be getting what they want.

But over time this arrangement can become less agreeable for a girl, because as the sex becomes more important and frequent, the relationship gets less and less attention. Like an unbalanced playground teeter-totter, sex sits as the heavier end while the relationship is suspended in midair, going nowhere. Teen dating activities such as hanging out, watching movies, studying, and going places together or in groups are replaced by sex. She used to have a dating relationship. Now he wants to pick her up at 9:00 and have her home by 9:15.

As the relationship shrinks and the sex grows, the inevitable happens: she becomes unhappy with him and the relationship. I've talked to many girls in dating relationships over the years, and a common refrain I have heard is "What happened to him? He used to be so nice." Usually the boy is nice. But he no longer shows it because sex has overtaken the relationship. And when sex takes over the relationship, the myth blows up. Despite what many young women believe, sex before marriage doesn't really make a relationship better; it supplants the relationship. It is then incumbent on us parents to help our daughters get to this core truth of sex and dating. In that spirit here are some things you can do to prepare your daughter to respond properly when she has to make a choice about sex in her relationship.

PREPARING YOUR DAUGHTER FOR FUTURE HAPPINESS
EDUCATE HER ABOUT SEX

Jacquelyn:
When I was somewhere around late elementary school, my mom took me out to breakfast at a local diner and drew a rough sketch of the female reproductive system on the back of her checkbook. She was frank, not weird about it, and I entered adolescence with the right information. The next day at school, I felt so enlightened! It seemed like I was in control; I understood my body. I was somehow head and shoulders above my peers. I felt empowered! This scary, mysterious thing was suddenly brought to light. The dreaded "period" was not so scary anymore.

When you have this conversation with your daughter, I recommend you do the following:

1. Talk in a neutral location where she cannot escape. The car, a restaurant, a place where she is forced to listen. My mom really hit the nail on the head with the restaurant idea.

2. Tell her about periods—everything about periods (Hey, guess what? They are normal, nothing to be scared of)—uterus function, pain associated with sex and menstrual cycle, and the layout of male and female sex organs and body parts.

3. Do the talking. Your daughter will probably want nothing to do with this conversation, so you're going to have to carry the ball. Even if she seems bored or exasperated with you, you can bet she is all ears. I spent that breakfast sitting and pushing my crepe around my plate, but I was listening.

4. Be chill. Seriously, chill out. Your daughter is just as weirded out by this as you are. Make sure that this is an adult conversation. Offer her a Coke, sit down, try to relax. One of my favorite things about my awesome mom is that no question freaks her out. She is very matter of fact and gives me the right information.

5. You might need a visual: drawings or photographs. Nothing about this topic should be a mystery or scary to your daughter. My mom used the back of a checkbook, but she is a very good artist. There are all sorts of resources on the Internet just for this purpose.

6. Leave the door open. Try to end this talk by making sure your daughter knows that she can talk to you about sex at

any time. About once a year, my mom would circle back around to this conversation—whether it had to do with my getting a year older or my getting into a new relationship.

EXPLAIN THE DIFFERENCES BETWEEN HOW GIRLS AND BOYS VIEW SEX

I know this is really awkward, but, dads, have you ever talked candidly with your daughter about boys and sex? Have you spoken truth into your daughter's life about the differences between boys and girls? Who better to hear about boys than from a man? Girls talk endlessly among themselves, dissecting every small word or move their boyfriends make. The reality is that your daughter doesn't understand at all the workings of the male brain. Tell her more about what it is like to be a boy. If she doesn't learn about these differences from you, where will she hear them?

Jacquelyn:
Your daughter needs to know that having sex to feel special and powerful will not make her so. If she is having sex to feel special, she isn't really special; she is just available. Send her the repeated message that what makes her special is the use of her power, choice, and force of will to be exceptional.

Feelings of self-worth and empowerment don't come from having a relationship or from having sex. They come from living an exceptional life. An exceptional life looks different from person to person, but I believe it is a life that is lived in service to others and brings honor to God and family. When we live this way, it is difficult not to feel empowered and valuable.

HELP HER UNDERSTAND WHY MARRIED SEX IS BEST

Research studies consistently show that married women have the most satisfying sex lives.[15] Why are women in committed marriages having the best sex? Because they are *making love* in the context of fulfilling relationships, not just *having sex*. More to the point, they are living out God's plan for sexual intimacy. It is crucial that your daughter understands that sex in the context of marriage is entirely different from sex outside of marriage.

When I asked Margaret, a friend who has been married for over fifty years to Rollie, how a healthy sex life has enhanced her marriage, she said, "It made me feel closer to him, cared for, loved, and needed." I'm sure many moms reading this book can echo a similar sentiment to Margaret's. I think it is of particular importance that moms teach daughters (and sons!) that what makes a relationship better is more *relationship*, not more sex.

If teenage girls view sex as the heart of a relationship, that can take them to some very ugly places. This is something we will explore in the next chapter, but for now, there are plenty of questions to be answered and discussions to be had from this chapter.

QUESTIONS FOR REFLECTION

1. What discussions have you had with your daughter about sex?
2. What have you told your daughter about why boys want to have sex?

3. In what ways does your daughter feel valuable? How have you told her specifically that she is valuable? Have you elaborated on this affirmation and not just given her a vague "You are a special girl"?

QUESTIONS FOR YOU AND YOUR DAUGHTER TO DISCUSS

1. Do you have friends who are sexually active? What do you think are their motivations for having sex? Are they healthy motivations?
2. What are the long-term consequences of being sexually active? (Think beyond just what you have learned in health class.) How might your future relationships be affected?
3. Do you know any girls whose first sexual experience was non-consensual? How has that changed them? How can you prevent this from happening to you?
4. Who would you tell if you were ever sexually assaulted?
5. What are the differences between why girls want to have sex and why boys want to have sex?

LOOKING AHEAD TO THE NEXT CHAPTER

Before a girl starts having sex, she believes it will enhance her relationship. As we have just read, there are plenty of reasons to suggest this notion is false. However, once a young girl is sexually active and experiencing sex in an immature relationship, she can feel trapped. The feelings of dissatisfaction can be difficult to reconcile with her feelings of love. Because of this paradox, she has to begin to believe dating myth #5: *Love and sex are the same.*

Dating Myth #5

Love and Sex Are the Same

Many years ago I was teaching, and while the students were working independently on a project in class, a sophomore girl sat down at my desk to check her grade. Some of the most serious discussions I've ever had with teens have occurred in a classroom full of students working busily away. She had been in my class for only a few weeks since her recent move to town.

As we talked, I asked her how she was adjusting to life in a new school and town. She said she was doing very well and was happy with her new boyfriend. I asked her who she was dating, and she told me his name was Zach. As soon as she said "Zach," it was as if a needle had been dragged across a vinyl record circa 1981. As a teacher I've had to make dozens and dozens of gut-instinct evaluations about when I should intervene with a student and when I should call a parent. The line is often fuzzy, and many times the parents are the root of the problem. Sometimes I hold information in confidence; other times I will tell a parent. Occasionally, I am legally obligated as a teacher to report what I hear. But in every case I am guided by what I think is in the best interest of the student *in that very moment*. And in that particular moment all I could think was *We have a major problem here*.

The problem was Zach. As a teacher I hear a lot, sometimes more than I'd like. I knew Zach had been in relationship after relationship and usually with the most vulnerable and needy girls. He had a reputation of dating eighth graders even though he was a high school junior. It would not have been an overstatement to say Zach was predatory. Everything I knew about him suggested to me this girl should not be dating him. I was fairly certain she had no idea what she had gotten herself into.

So I began to ask her about her relationship.

"How long have you been dating Zach?"

"For about a month," she replied.

"How are you getting along?"

"Great. Zach is sweet and really nice. He's a great boyfriend," she said enthusiastically.

With mounting concern I asked, "Are you pretty serious about him?"

"Yes, I really love him."

Now, I knew Zach's method of operation, and I was sure there was no way Zach was in love with her. So it was time for me to ask a few more questions.

"Have you introduced him to your mom?"

"No," she said with not too much concern.

I pressed for more information and asked, "Have you met his family or any of his friends?"

"No," she said again, without much care.

"Has he met any of your family or friends?"

"No," she replied. Only now she was sensing I was up to something with all these questions.

"Have you ever been out on a date?" I asked with ever-more-increasing concern.

"No."

"So where do you go when you are together?" I asked, though I already knew the answer.

"We just hang out at my house," she said.

I was one step ahead of her, and I knew this "relationship" was not going nearly as well as she believed. She and Zach had never met each other's families, yet they were spending so much time together that she thought she was in love. Hmm. So more questions, but this time with additional seriousness.

"When do you see Zach?"

"He comes over at night."

Uh-oh, I thought. *She knows I am up to something, but she still doesn't know what.* "What time does he come over?"

"Usually late. Like around eleven or twelve." Still, with not much concern on her part.

"That's kind of late. How does he get in your house?" I said, even though I already knew the answer.

"He comes in through my bedroom window."

At this point I pretty much knew the score. Zach was hitting home runs with this girl, and she had no idea that she was just another girl at bat in his scorecard. She was having sex with him, likely soon to be crushed emotionally, and worse yet she was at risk for pregnancy. This was a desperate time for her, so it called for desperate measures.

With the greatest delicacy I could muster, I asked, "You don't have to answer this question if you don't want to, but are you having sex with him?"

"Mr. Anderson!" she said with a quiet embarrassment as she looked to the ground.

"No, really. Are you having sex with him?"

"Yes," she said as sheepishly as an eight-year-old caught in a lie.

"Did you have sex with him the first night?" Again, I figured I already knew the answer.

Even more sheepishly than before she said, "Yes."

Knowing Zach's predatory reputation, I decided to tell her what was going on. "I have some really bad news. You are the midnight girl." (The word *booty call* was not in use in 1994, when this conversation occurred, but it would have applied just as well.) "Zach has a 9:00 p.m. girl and maybe even a 3:00 a.m. girl. You are not the only girl he is with. Think about it. You have never been seen in public with him. What does that mean to you?"

Her face went pale and her jaw kind of went slack. In a tone of ignorance, resignation, and incredulity, she said, "Really?"

We talked for quite a while longer that day. She was crushed. As tears streamed down her cheeks, she admitted she had no idea what was going on. It was a painful lesson for her to learn. We talked at length about how she needed to break up with Zach. She was reeling and didn't know if she wanted to break up with him because she still "loved him."

Again, desperate times called for desperate measures. Because her grade was in need of help, I said this: "I'll give you fifty points extra credit if you call Zach right now and break up with him."

"I don't know, Mr. Anderson ..."

"We can walk right down to the pay phone in center hall, and you can call him right now. Here, I even have a quarter," I said as pulled a Washington from my pocket.

It took a few more minutes of convincing, but she was soon on the phone cursing a blue streak and breaking up with Zach. She uttered my name a few times, and I'm sure to this day Zach would probably like to punch me in the throat. But on that day my mission was accomplished. A life was changed.

There is truly never a dull day as a high school teacher! I'm happy to report that this girl got more help from the school counselor and she never got back together with Zach.

As you read that story, I'm sure most of you thought the same thing: *How could that poor girl get herself into that mess? Where was her sense of value? How could she have possibly thought she was in love?* Those are all good questions for which I don't have easy answers. But I do know this. She confused love and sex, and she thought Zach was reciprocating her feelings of love. She also mistakenly believed that the thoughts in her head were identical to the thoughts in his.

This student is not too different from a lot of girls today. Many are in relationships in which they are little more than short-term drive-bys for the boys they are dating. These girls would tell you they are way different from Zach's girlfriend. They are smarter, more experienced, and more prepared than she was. But the sad fact remains, many teen girls confuse sex with love.

Jacquelyn:
I saw this confusion over and over among my high school friends (and continue to see it in my twentysomething girlfriends). Most girls just don't understand that while the girl feels connected during sex, the boy just feels superawesome in that moment. I had a girlfriend in high

school whose boyfriend had sex with at least five different girls while he was dating her. Even when she found out the truth, she stayed with him! In her mind, she was the "main" girlfriend and the other girls were just "booty calls." In reality, she was just another drive-by. There is a reason why people quote statistics as evidence. (My dad does this all the time in this book.) Most people are the rule, not the exception. While there is a minuscule chance that the guy a teenage girl is having sex with loves her, it's much more likely that he does not.

HOW GIRLS COME TO SEE SEX AS LOVE

How does this happen? How do girls come to equate sex with love? After all, everyone knows love and sex are different. We say it all the time. Sex and love have been largely bifurcated in Hollywood. I wonder how many times a year the words "I love you" are uttered in Hollywood productions versus the number of times two characters have sex? The rise of porn culture further communicates to teens that love and sex are different. (And if you doubt that porn has gone mainstream, just ask yourself how Kim Kardashian's sex tape helped make her a "star" and why Howard Stern's experience interviewing porn stars makes him a good candidate to be a judge on a family variety show.)

Teenage girls often understand intellectually that love and sex are different—and many say they want to wait until they are in love to have sex. However, many of them don't *act* as if they understand the difference.

So how does a girl move from an intellectual understanding that love and sex are different to an emotional understanding that love and sex are the same? Once again the answer is found in gender differences between boys and girls. We discussed in the previous chapter that an emotionally healthy girl will want to have sex as an extension of her feelings for her boyfriend. The desire for intimate connection causes her to choose to be sexually active. She has love and gives sex. But the sex she is experiencing is less than it should be.

As adults we may understand that sex was designed by God to be about intimacy, sharing, commitment, closeness, and a host of emotions that support mutually satisfying sex lives in the context of marriage. When sex is experienced outside of this plan, sexually active girls begin to understand that the intimacy and closeness they felt when they first had sex were largely counterfeit. As a result, they don't feel special and loved anymore. The erosion of this emotional connection leaves them feeling cheap and used. In order to not feel cheap and used, girls have to perform a curious feat of mental and emotional gymnastics.

Jacquelyn:
Just a few paragraphs ago I mentioned my friend who stayed with her boyfriend even after learning he was sleeping with other girls. Talk about mental gymnastics! I remember it so vividly. Several other friends and I sat her down in front of her locker and told her everything. "He's a cheater. He's disgusting. He doesn't love you." She cried, we cried, and then the next day we saw her holding his hand in the hallway. She had convinced herself that he wasn't a bad guy, that he needed just a little bit of help. I

see this kind of crazy logic all the time in high school girls. It doesn't make any sense, yet girls make decisions based on this faulty thinking all the time.

Psychologists call this mental backflip *dissonance reduction*. When a person has two inconsistent ideas about himself or herself, it creates dissonance. This dissonance is often reduced through rationalization. In this case a girl believes she is not cheap and easy. But at the same time, the lack of emotional connection she feels when having sex with her boyfriend leaves her feeling cheap and easy. How can she reconcile these two opposing ideas? By believing that love and sex are the same. She knows something is missing in the relationship—namely, the relationship. So instead of the relationship being the gauge for measuring the depth of her boyfriend's love, sex becomes the gauge. Because if the sex is not love, then just what is she other than a one-night stand?

WHY SHE THINKS HE LOVES HER

By the time a girl reaches her midteens, she understands a great deal about teenage boys. She knows they don't bathe regularly. (After teaching freshman boys for nearly twenty years, I can attest to that!) She knows they are way more aggressive and get in fights more easily than girls. She knows they really like sex and think about it all the time. She is fully aware that boys like to look at girls. She knows they are way stronger than girls and can be a little scary. But what she doesn't always understand is that what she is feeling is much different from what a boy is feeling.

One reason for this, I suspect, is because teenage boys don't talk about their feelings. When I'm counseling a student about a personal issue, I typically ask him or her, "How do you feel about all this?" Girls have much to say when asked this question. Boys, however, usually look at me in stony silence. If I reframe the question for a boy to "What do you think you should do about this?" I often get a much more engaged response. If I can turn an emotional process into a cognitive process, boys do much better.

In the absence of information about how a boy is feeling, teenage girls assume he is much like they are. They think boys have the same rich and complex emotional lives they do; it's just that boys don't talk about it. But this isn't the case. I know because I work with teenage boys every day.

The danger of this misunderstanding is compounded when a boy tells a girl "I love you." When she says "I love you" to him, she means something entirely different from when he says "I love you" to her. But she doesn't pick up on that.

Jacquelyn:

When I try to describe being a teenager to people, I often refer to what I call the "imaginary fishbowl." In adolescence, I sometimes had this creeping feeling that everyone was watching me, criticizing me, when in fact, no one really was. I was hypercritical and aware of myself in a way that was irrational. Because of this, I had a hard time understanding that anyone's brain—let alone my boyfriend's—could work differently than my own. I was too focused on me to think critically about what was going on with him.

In child development there is a stage at which small children understand that their thoughts are different from the thoughts of others. This is called theory of mind.[1] It is as if when a boy tells a girl "I love you" she no longer has theory of mind. She mistakenly believes his feelings are identical to hers and that her love is being returned in the same measure. She doesn't understand that his words mean something different to him than they do to her.

To better understand why, we need to return to our discussion of how the male brain differs from the female brain.

MORE BRAIN DIFFERENCES BETWEEN GENDERS

In the last chapter we discussed the straightforward nature of male sexual desire: it's largely visual and opportunistic. A boy's testosterone levels dictate much of his desire for sex. While female desire is steeped in emotional intimacy, male sexual desire lies elsewhere. In another example of this difference between genders, one study shows that 53 percent of college men would have sex without kissing, yet only 14 percent of college women would do the same.[2] For most females, kissing is an intimate act that is integral to sex, but that's not the case for the majority of males.

The reason for this divide lies in the differences between the male and female limbic systems—the part of the brain that is central in emotional processing. Brain imaging confirms that females have larger limbic systems than males do.[3] This explains why girls are more in touch with their feelings than boys are.

I've observed this difference close up and on a broad scale in the classroom. A few times over the years I've asked students to write down a list of emotions they feel regularly. The lists that girls create are spectacular. They contain words such as *despondent, dejected, forlorn, lonely, blue, upset, enraged,* and so on. The lists boys create are short and simple. They will say something that sounds like this: "Uh … happy … uh … mad … uh … and horny." (Hey, that's not even an emotion!)

Because they have larger limbic systems, girls are also better at intimacy and bonding than boys are. (This may in part explain why you would be hard pressed to find a society in which men are the primary caretakers of children.) This greater capacity for bonding and intimacy is part and parcel of female sexual desire. But because boys have a more limited capacity for intimacy and bonding, they are unable to experience intimate bonding to the level most girls want.

Another element to consider is the delayed brain development of boys when compared to girls. Though the numbers vary by researcher, it is safe to say female brain development is complete by the early twenties. However, male brain development may not finish until the age of thirty.[4] Girls mature earlier and faster than boys do. This includes the smooth meshing of emotional and cognitive processes. As a result, a young man just isn't feeling what a young woman is.

Jacquelyn:

I once had an English teacher who had our class spend a whole month studying love poems. We read Shakespeare, Pablo Neruda, and countless others. I loved it and so did my best friend. Our classroom discussions were lively. Then one day our teacher stopped dead in her tracks and announced that no more girls could talk until two boys had shared their thoughts on the poem we were discussing. Cue the crickets in that room! We had been talking about all the nuance of emotion, tone, and diction while the boys in the class were just counting the minutes until the bell rang.

My own experience reflects this. Tamara and I married fairly young. I was twenty-three and she was twenty-one. The early years of our marriage were difficult for me because Tamara was so much more emotionally aware than I was. There were things she was experiencing and feeling early in our marriage that I was completely unaware of. This led to some considerable frustration on her part. It wasn't until Jacquelyn was born that I began to grow emotionally. Feelings I did not know even existed were suddenly surging through me. As I've gotten older, I've become more sensitive and insightful with my emotional life. Though I don't think I will ever catch up to my wife, I am in middle age far more emotionally complex than I was as a young man.

What all this means for our daughters is that the depth of emotional connection and love they may be feeling for their boyfriends is likely not reciprocal. The average teenage boy simply isn't capable of feeling the depth or intensity of emotions that a girl feels. His brain is not developed and mature enough. While he may have very strong feelings for his girlfriend, they are substantially more shallow and underdeveloped than hers are. But if she doesn't pick up on this, a girl may stay in the relationship, putting herself in a very vulnerable position for heartache.

When a girl enters into a sexual relationship with a boy, she exchanges something of value. In exchange for his "love," she gives him everything. She shares her most intimate self, both physically and emotionally. She gives him her full trust. She gives away her time and freedom. What does she get in return? More often than not she gets heartache.

WHY THIS SHOULD ALARM YOU

When she confuses love and sex, a girl believes even more that she is experiencing the deep love of attachment and will invest far too much of herself in a relationship far too soon. The danger of this for a young girl is that when sex replaces love, there is a mixing of hedonic and goal-centered happiness. For married people, one of their goals in life is usually a harmonious and fulfilling marriage. Most adults understand that a satisfying marriage is much more than sex. While a part of marriage, sex is not the totality of marriage. But when sex and love are tied together, sex can become the totality of the relationship. If relationship goals such as intimacy, communication, and shared vision are replaced by the hedonic goal of sex, then sex becomes the barometer of the relationship. And how does this make the girl feel? Used.

Even worse, if sex is love, it means the boy loves the girl, right? And if so, then that means his other behaviors are secondary indicators of his love. He doesn't call and text regularly? That's okay, because the love is in the sex. He doesn't make her feel special when they are together? That's okay, because the love is in the sex. He flirts with other girls? That's okay, because the love is in the sex. He yells at her? That's okay, because the love is in the sex. He pushes and hits her? That's okay, because the love is in the sex. If a girl comes to believe that sex is the goal and measure of happiness, then she can put herself into unhealthy situations that can compromise her future happiness.

At the beginning of this chapter I told the story of the young woman who was "dating" Zach and how she had confused love and sex. While it may seem to be an impossible story to believe, I will tell you that nearly any girl might be prone to confusing love and sex—including your own daughter! This fact makes the rest of this chapter critically important.

PREPARING YOUR DAUGHTER FOR FUTURE HAPPINESS

TALK WITH HER ABOUT HOW MALES AND FEMALES PROCESS EMOTIONS

If at all possible, have Mom and Dad sit together and explain to your daughter how you both process emotions differently. If the other parent is unavailable, get another adult of the opposite gender to assist. I would focus on specific emotions such as love, fear, anger, and frustration. I believe it will be invaluable for your daughter to hear that men and women are emotionally different.

EDUCATE HER ABOUT THE DIFFERENCES IN THE MALE AND FEMALE BRAINS

Encourage her to read some excerpts from Dr. Louann Brizendine's books *The Female Brain* and *The Male Brain*. Both of these books do an exceptional job at highlighting the uniqueness of the male and female brains. This information will help both you and your daughter to understand how different the genders are.

After reading chapter 2 of *The Female Brain*, "Teen Girl Brain," you and your daughter will be able to explore further some of the topics this book briefly touches on: puberty, the role of estrogen and progesterone in regulating emotions, dopamine and the reward system, and the role of oxytocin in relationship formation. *The Male Brain* is equally enlightening. It contains great insight into gender differences between boys and girls. By reading through this book with your daughter, you can help her understand just how different boys are when it comes to verbal processing, risk-taking behaviors, facial recognition, and perhaps most important, the nature of sexual desire.

BECOME A WATERING HOLE FOR YOUR DAUGHTER

Anna Creek Station in Australia is the largest ranch in the world. It covers ninety-four hundred square miles, which is slightly larger than the state of New Hampshire.[5] One of the problems of having such a large ranch is, how do you keep the cattle from wandering off? I did a quick Google search and learned that cattle fencing costs about two dollars a linear foot.[6] To fence the entire Anna Creek Station cattle ranch would cost approximately $2 million, which makes it impractical and too costly for cattle ranchers to fence in their herds. So they dig watering holes—deep, life-giving, thirst-quenching watering holes. The watering holes keep the cattle from wandering off the ranch.

The range of our daughters' lives might as well be as big as Anna Creek Station. Chances are good that they will wander too far from the ranch, putting too much trust in their feelings and losing sight of what's important. As parents we don't want our daughters to wander off the ranch. Some parents try to build fences to keep their kids on the ranch. But there is not enough fencing in the world to keep our daughters from venturing out. (Believe me, I tried!) Other parents don't bother with fences at all. They let their daughters wander and just hope they don't go too far away. The problem with these approaches is neither works very well. What works? Watering holes.

If you want your daughter to date smart, avoid disaster, and protect her future, be a watering hole that is full of love and she will turn to you when she is thirsty. The things you have taught her about dating will be the water she returns to when she is wandering. Her understanding of her own goodness and value will be water as well.

You have likely heard the phrase "It takes a whole village to raise a child." I'm not sure most adults truly understand what that means, but as a high school teacher I understand. It means that there will be times when a parent is just not enough. Despite your best efforts and intentions, your daughter needs other sane and rational adults in her life who will say the same exact things you're saying. The only difference is that they will be people other than Mom and Dad saying them. That just might do the trick. As you work to help your daughter understand that love and sex are different, surround her with adults who have the same understanding as you, whether it be a supportive teacher, pastor, rabbi, or other trusted adult. Working together, you and the community of adults surrounding your daughter can help her understand clearly that love and sex are different.

QUESTIONS FOR REFLECTION

1. Have you ever confused love and sex? What can you tell your daughter about this?

2. What have you taught your daughter about how love and sex can be confused?

3. How are you raising your daughter with an understanding of gender differences?

4. How are you modeling a loving relationship for your daughter and healthy attitudes toward sex?

QUESTIONS FOR YOU AND YOUR DAUGHTER TO DISCUSS

1. Why do you think a girl would confuse sex and love?

2. How are boys' feelings about sex different from girls' feelings about sex?

3. What impact do you think the media has on your attitudes regarding sex?

4. How are boys more immature than girls at your age?

LOOKING AHEAD TO THE NEXT CHAPTER

When love and sex are the same, the relationships go too far too soon at a time in a girl's life when she is too young to understand the implications. As the sex grows and the relationship shrinks, she begins to take tremendous risks physically, emotionally, and with regard to her future. But she moves ahead oblivious to this because she believes dating myth #6: *Sex comes without consequences.*

Sex Comes without Consequences

This may be the hardest sentence I will write in this book:

Your daughter may be having sex.

If the research is to be believed, by the age of nineteen roughly 70 percent of American teens have had sex.[1] Every parent wants to think his or her daughter is the exception to the rule. And in some cases she is the exception to the rule, but more often, she is the rule. The likelihood of this is a mathematical probability.

Your daughter is growing up in a hypersexualized culture with ever-shifting mores regarding sex. If you want to avoid disaster and protect her future happiness, then you can't be an ostrich around this reality. You need to believe that she may already be where you don't want her to be.

If there is one thing I've learned over my years as a schoolteacher, it is that every teen has a secret life. I had a secret life. My siblings had secret lives. My own children have secret lives.

I'm willing to bet you had a secret life too (and maybe you still do). Why should your daughter be any different from you and nearly every other teenager who has ever lived? The difficult truth is that your daughter may be, or may soon be, sexually active.

And if so, she probably believes that she can have sex without consequences. If she has any qualms about having sex, she will likely tell herself, *Everybody is doing it. How can it be so bad?* As parents we need to set the record straight.

In order to understand why your daughter might believe this myth, you'll find it helpful to know how sex education has evolved over the years.

THE FAILURE OF HEALTH 101 AND OF ABSTINENCE EDUCATION

In 1940 the US Public Health Service declared an "urgent need" for sex education in America.[2] The emphasis on sex education in public schools continued after World War II and gained momentum throughout the 1950s and '60s. For decades teachers have taught the importance of safe sex and birth control. Today, sex education curriculum is a politically and ideologically charged topic with multiple stakeholders pressing various agendas. Amid the din, what comes across loud and clear to teenage girls is that sex is primarily a biological act with few emotional consequences.

The "National Sexuality Education Standards," a report completed in 2012, recommends that sex educators teach twenty-two core concepts as part of health classes nationwide. These concepts contain information on bullying, gender, sexual orientation, birth control, safe sex, sexual coercion, and more. Eleven of them have to do with the biology of sex and gender; seven deal with legal issues in human sexuality. The other four are spread out over brain development, healthy role models, and healthy relationships. What these core concepts fail to address are fundamental questions about readiness for sex, emotional consequences of sex, and the implications of teen sex on future marital stability.[3] Yet these are the consequences our daughters really need to know about. The message teens need to hear is that sex is far more than just biology.

Comprehensive sex education has been the norm in America for nearly six decades, but the facts tell us that it hasn't been effective in keeping kids from having sex. The average American loses his or her virginity around age seventeen.[4] While teen pregnancy rates have fallen to historic lows,[5] the US teen pregnancy rate is higher than the rates in Austria, Australia, Belgium, Canada, France, Germany, Ireland, Portugal, Spain, Sweden, Switzerland, and the United Kingdom.[6] At twenty-four births per one thousand teen girls, the United States has the highest teen birthrate of any industrialized country in the world. Though fifteen- to twenty-four-year-olds are only one-quarter of the sexually active population, they account for more than one-half of the new sexually transmitted infections (STIs) each year.[7]

Many Christians see abstinence-only education as the answer to risky teen sexual behavior. However, the effectiveness of the increase in abstinence or abstinence-only curricula within sex education courses has shown mixed results.[8] One study even suggests abstinence-only education is positively correlated with higher teen pregnancy rates.[9]

Jacquelyn:

The extent of our abstinence education at my high school was simply, the Bible says don't do, so don't. Of course our teachers talked about STIs and the possibility of pregnancy, but they never mentioned the emotional and spiritual consequences. This approach wasn't nearly as effective as our parents and teachers wanted to believe. Some of the couples in my Christian school were sexually active, despite being told sex outside of marriage was wrong. I would say somewhere around 25 percent, but it was kept pretty secret around the school, so it was likely higher. Why the disparity between our behavior and what we were taught? Because in the heat of the moment, few girls are willing to say to their boyfriends, "Sorry. We need to back up. I don't want to do this. My youth pastor says it's a sin." The pressure to conform, combined with the desire to have sex, is simply too great for most kids to abstain from sex when they are on the brink.

What I think girls need to hear is the consequences above and beyond what they are taught in sex ed. How will having sex make them feel in the long run? How will it affect the rest of their lives? What are healthy motivations for wanting to have sex? Why is marriage such a perfect setting for sex? What happens when you break up with someone whom you've had sex with?

The aim of this book is not to wade into the sex education debate. But this much is clear: regardless of ideology, sex education has been largely ineffective in changing teenage behavior.

INACCURATE PORTRAYALS FROM THE CULTURE

Another reason a girl can believe sex comes without consequences is because of how sex is portrayed in popular culture. Consider the countless sex acts on TV, showing couples having sex amid soft sheets, burning candles, and blissful delight. According to the most recent publication on the topic of sex and TV from the Kaiser Family Foundation, the number of shows featuring sex continues to rise.[10] Song lyrics and music videos can be downright pornographic and further communicate that sex is always deeply satisfying. Be it movies, TV, or music, we don't see much of the negative side of sex— consequences such as pregnancy, STIs, and emotional pain.

But as we've seen in the last two chapters, most of the media's portrayal of sex is contrary to what a sexually active teenage girl experiences. Her experience of sex is only a cheap fake compared to the way sex was designed to work. It lacks both the physical pleasure and the emotional connectedness of sex the way it should be experienced—in the confines of a communicative, mature, and loving marriage relationship.

When a girl's physical and emotional needs go unmet when she has sex, she feels used and empty. For some, the mental backflip of the previous chapter—that love and sex are the same—is an effective remedy for this problem. But in time this backflip no longer provides the intellectual cover for the feelings of shame she is experiencing. This is particularly true if a girl has multiple sex partners. What happens when a sexually active girl realizes that love and sex are not the same? She convinces herself that sex comes without consequences, thus minimizing the power of sex. Her belief in this dating myth enables her to view sex in a more casual light. If sex is not love, then it must be a mere biological act without larger consequences to consider.

The dangers of such an attitude are myriad. Let's take a closer look at some of the fallout that comes when girls believe they can have sex without consequences.

THE CONSEQUENCES OF BELIEVING SEX COMES WITHOUT CONSEQUENCES
HER BRAIN IMPRINTS FAULTY THINKING ABOUT SEX

I think every adult can recall how easy it was to learn new things when we were young. Music, sports, languages all come much easier in the developing brain. It is not just lack of spare time to acquire new skills that makes it so "old dogs can't learn new tricks." The brain of a teen is still developing, and thus it has greater plasticity than the adult brain and is more primed for learning. Scientists believe that as a brain matures, neural connections that are not used wither and die. It is a "use it or lose it" proposition, and those neural connections that are used begin to hardwire.[11] In other words, *the behaviors and attitudes of the teen years become the imprinted ways of an adult.* Wow! The implications of this are good and bad.

On the good end of the spectrum is the fact that as parents we have the opportunity to help our children develop healthy attitudes and behaviors that will be hardwired into their brains. When we consistently expect and encourage patterns of behavior that our children may think of as mundane—completing homework, keeping clean rooms, participating in family chores, and so forth—we are preparing our kids to be responsible and successful adults. The same is true regarding more meaningful behaviors and attitudes that we want cemented into our children's hearts—qualities such as compassion, responsibility, and self-discipline. Just as important, if we help our children to have healthy attitudes and behaviors about sex, these are also getting hardwired into their brains.

On the bad end of the spectrum is the fact that unhealthy attitudes and behaviors get imprinted as well. This is why the attitudes and behaviors that our teenage daughters are developing with regard to sex are so critical.

What is the overall message that sexually active teen girls are learning about sex? That sex is mostly for him and it isn't all that special. In coaching and teaching it is said that "perfect practice makes perfect." Because teen sex is a mere shadow of what it is supposed to be in a mature, lifetime relationship, what actually is happening for a teen girl is that "imperfect practice makes imperfect." The more sexual partners a young girl has, the more her brain is imprinting that imperfect practice. How is she supposed to learn to be vulnerable and trusting with her sexuality in this context? Sex is supposed to help sustain marriages for decades. But how can it when it has been cheapened and diminished through imperfect practice?

In earlier chapters we discussed the role of oxytocin in social bonding and physical pleasure. Numerous studies have confirmed that oxytocin also plays a significant role in the formation of trust.[12] In fact, oxytocin is often called the trust hormone. When a girl is in a relationship, physical intimacy produces large amounts of oxytocin that facilitate trust. This may in part explain why girls confuse sex and love.[13] The feelings of trust created by oxytocin are short lived but profoundly important. These trust feelings, when juxtaposed against the reality of feeling used and empty, leave a girl hopelessly confused. She "trusts" again and again through sex, but ends up feeling hurt. When a girl's trust has been violated, she is likely to withhold trust in future relationships in order to avoid the anticipated hurt. She avoids heartache by investing less of herself emotionally. She avoids pain by downplaying the power of sex by believing it comes without consequences.

Jacquelyn:

Every girl knows a girl with a laissez-faire attitude toward sex and relationships. All of her jokes, stories, and comments are sexualized in a way that masks a lot of pain in that area. Mine was a friend in high school named Abby. Abby would become interested in a boy, then quickly round the bases, making sex the focus of the relationship. Despite the physical intimacy, her boyfriends didn't seem to know anything about her. She was allergic to peanuts, and one of them gave her a Reese's cup for Valentine's Day!

Abby and I were both TAs at the same time. We spent countless hours talking in the school copy room. While I didn't realize it then, it is clear to me now that Abby had confused love and sex and had shut down emotionally to avoid being hurt. She was addicted to the oxytocin but chose to avoid the pain by trivializing sex in both her words and her actions. I have kept in contact with Abby, and she is a tremendously unhappy young woman. In college she was always the drunkest girl at the bar and often went home with a stranger. She would laugh and wink, but you could always see that sadness behind her eyes. She recently had a child, and her boyfriend left her when their daughter was only six months old. Her relationship patterns were ones that were formed in her teenage years, and she cannot shake them in her twenties.

If a girl imprints unhealthy attitudes and behaviors concerning sex, those patterns can bedevil her for decades to come and play out in her future relationships.

In *Surprised by the Healer*, a book by Linda Dillow and Dr. Juli Slattery about sexual healing, "Marian" writes what she learned about sex from her teen relationships:

> I was fifteen when my older boyfriend ignored me when I told him no. I looked at the clock when he started, and then again when he finished. Six minutes to womanhood. All the while I could hear cheers coming from the other side of the closed door.
>
> Afterward, he took me out to fast food so we could talk.
>
> "If you get pregnant or something, I'll pay to have it taken care of."
>
> "What?"
>
> "I'll pay for an abortion."
>
> I hadn't thought of that. "Oh."
>
> We ate a little more in silence.
>
> "And there's one more thing."
>
> I looked up at him, trying to sift through everything that had happened, trying to redefine our relationship now that we'd had sex.

"I don't think we're working out," he said between bites.

My entire teenage world came crashing down through the smell of garlic bread sticks and ready-made ravioli.

Within the month, he was dating someone else. They went to church together. I heard she had told him no, and he had listened.

The lies I embraced:

I am disposable.

My nakedness might be repulsive.

The next guy I dated never talked unless he was drinking. As soon as he was drunk, he was all hands and demands. Still, he didn't leave me after the first night we had sex. During our year of dating, I learned the lie that *substances create a numbness that should be part of the sexual experience....*

At twenty-two, I met and married Nathan, a pastor, no less.

Despite my newfound faith and Nathan's love, my attitude toward sex was hardened. I believed I was just a product; I could be discarded, traded for someone more desirable, or consumed and left empty.[14]

I'm sure many people reading this book can identify unhealthy patterns of behavior that started in their teen years. With your encouragement and support, your daughter can hardwire healthy attitudes and beliefs about sex.

SHE CAN DEVELOP A GROWING RESENTMENT TOWARD MALES

When a girl is being used over and over again by a boy, how could she help but feel resentment? And why shouldn't she? She is only an object for gratification. And because the sex she is experiencing lacks emotional connectedness, she feels like she isn't really a whole person. One author put resentment this way: "Resentment is the persistent feeling that you are being treated unfairly—not getting due respect, appreciation, affection.... It keeps you locked in a devalued state, wherein it is extremely difficult to improve or appreciate or connect positively with people in general."[15]

Another researcher, Michael Linden, has proposed a mental illness diagnosis called post-traumatic embitterment disorder (PTED). According to Linden, those suffering from PTED have a triggering event that challenges their core values and basic beliefs. This challenge to the core value system leaves a person feeling embittered and often vengeful.[16] It is my observation that for many young women engaging in premarital sex, it presents a challenge to their core belief that they are a good and valuable person. Feeling used on a regular basis may cause a teen girl to end up feeling embittered, particularly after a breakup. In my opinion, the shock of a breakup and the regret regarding physical intimacy are very traumatizing and can leave a girl very angry. An embittered young woman may carry this resentment into future relationships. This is hardly a good starting point for a healthy lifetime relationship, and consequently, she puts her future relationships in peril.

SHE STARTS HAVING SEX LIKE A MAN

In chapter 4 we discussed the fact that for most boys emotions and sexual desire exist apart from each other. At the same time, emotions and sexual desire in a healthy girl often go hand in hand. For sex to be truly without consequences, a girl has to operate more like a boy. She has to have sex with no emotional attachment. Despite her hardwiring for relational and emotional intimacy, a girl will try to override her own biology by bifurcating sex and emotion. She downplays the emotional consequences of sex and tries to be something she is not, namely, more like a boy. In today's vernacular, she "hooks up."

TODAY'S HOOKUP CULTURE

So just what is a "hookup"? To "hook up" means to have some form of sexual intimacy (anything from kissing to intercourse and anything in between) that is brief in nature (a few minutes to a single night) and is purely physical in nature.[17] In my day we would have called it a "one-night stand" or "noncommittal suckface." Today, it is called "friends with benefits" (FWB).

Many parents would be surprised to discover that the morality around premarital sex has changed dramatically in the last thirty years. Most people in their thirties and forties grew up with the belief that sex was supposed to be part of a relationship, usually the marriage relationship. I believe the following quote from a high school student typifies the new morality around sex: "I decided that mutual respect and some sort of caring—not necessarily love, just some compassionate feelings—are necessary for me to have sex with someone."

The bar has been lowered regarding what is required for the average teen girl to agree to have sex. I would argue that twenty-five years ago, many girls saw the first date as a path to a relationship and sexual intimacy. It would be the first of many dates that would evolve into an exclusive, dating relationship. However, the hookup culture has turned that idea upside down. In one study, college students reported twice as many hookups as first dates.[18] It seems to me that the modern teen now views a relationship as a by-product of sex. In another study, more than half of the three hundred college students queried at a large public university reported "hooking up" in the past year.[19] Hookup culture thrives on college campuses in America, where to be "sexually intimate means to become emotionally empty."[20] Part of the hookup culture is that students date less and engage in sexual activity with friends or someone they just met more often.[21]

HOOKING UP ON HIGH SCHOOL CAMPUSES

Unfortunately, the research is limited regarding hookup culture among high school students. But one researcher found that "70 percent of sexually active 12- to 21-year-olds reported having had uncommitted sex within the last year."[22] However, even though we don't have extensive research on this issue, it is pretty clear high school students are involved in hooking up. So as I prepared to write this section, I spoke with my two daughters and ten of my current or former female students to get an idea of hookup culture among high school students. It is one thing to read about and research on hookup culture; it is quite another to get unfiltered responses from young people you know well. I asked them:

Why are girls getting involved in hookup culture?

What role does alcohol play in hookups?

The responses I received confirmed much of what researchers and writers have to say on the topic.

WHY GIRLS HOOK UP

One central theme ran through these young women's responses to my question about why girls hook up: girls hook up to feel better about themselves. One young woman said, "Girls hook up to feel pretty and special." Another said, "Hookups are a status and attention thing." I discussed this comment with several of the girls, and remarkably, they agreed that the approval of the peer group is crucial for girls involved in hookups. The more boys a girl can hook up with, the higher her status in the group. Additionally, hooking up with the "hottest" guys will give her the most status. One girl said, "Hookups are similar to 'likes' on Facebook." She also noted that hookups are an extension of social media. Your status in the world of hookups is measured by the number of boys you are sexually intimate with, particularly if those boys are handsome and/or high on the social ladder. I can't imagine that a girl who really understood her value would ever measure her worth by the number of guys she hooked up with.

Several of the girls said another contributing factor to hookup culture is a misguided notion that having sex like a man is part of being equal to men. For many young women, to be equal to a man means gaining the ability to do all things men do. The idea of equal rights for women is an important one. It was foundational to the suffrage movement, the equal-rights movement of the 1970s,

Title IX legislation, and much more. However, this idea has been co-opted by society at large to mean women (girls) can do *anything* that men (boys) can do. One girl put it this way: "For some girls, hooking up feels like you are being a feminist."

For years people have rightly bristled at the traditional double standard that a man with many conquests is a "stud" but a girl engaged in the same behavior is a "slut." What's happened in the last decade is that the culture is now condemning "slut shaming." To "slut shame" means to "publicly or privately [insult] a woman because she expressed her sexuality in a way that does not conform with patriarchal expectations for women."[23] If men and women are truly equal, there should be no shame when either gender sleeps around. Sadly, nearly all the girls I spoke with said this practice is pervasive among many teenagers and that it is taboo for anyone to cast judgment on another girl's sexual activity. Many social commentators and critics hail this attitude as a "victory" in the war on discrimination against women. They think it is the height of female empowerment to sleep with anyone without judgment. If this is a victory, then it is a Pyrrhic one. I'm not sure encouraging girls to act as stupid and reckless as boys is a win.

THE ROLE OF ALCOHOL IN HOOKUPS

Part of acting like a man is also drinking like a man. While binge-drinking rates among young men have fallen in the last two decades, women's binge-drinking rates have remained steady.[24] When it comes to binge drinking, young men seem to be getting the message and girls are trying to be "one of the boys."

When I asked my high school students what role alcohol plays in hookups, the responses had a central theme: without alcohol hookup culture barely exists. One of the college students said, "Partying and hooking up is just the expected thing on campus." A high school student said, "Being drunk gives you an excuse … and it helps with awkwardness." One study confirms that 55 percent of all sexual encounters among college students with someone other than a steady partner involved alcohol.[25] I have no reason to believe that if the same survey were given to high school students the results would change.

One of the girls I spoke with noted that some of her peers pretend to be drunk in order to have an excuse for their behavior. She said, "They'll have like a sip of beer and say, 'Oh, I was drunk. I didn't know what I was doing.'" But sometimes students *are* too drunk to know what they are doing. The National Institutes of Health reported in a 2013 publication that "each year 100,000 students between the ages of 18 and 24 report having been too intoxicated to know if they consented to having sex."[26] Another smaller study conducted in Canada found that 71 percent of the college students who engaged in hookups were intoxicated.[27] I'm inclined to believe these sorts of findings would be just as true for students in high school.

Jacquelyn:
When I was in high school, we lived on the border of the rural side of Portland. Some of my friends lived on big parcels of land with barns, fire pits, and all sorts of ways to entertain ourselves on a Saturday night. Although I didn't

drink in high school, almost everyone I know experimented with alcohol at some point. I had a small group of acquaintances who spent every Friday and Saturday night getting rip-roaring drunk around a big bonfire. Many of the girls in this group lost their virginity. Others had sex with more than one person at these bonfires. These were pretty great girls! I remember getting breakfast with one such girlfriend the next morning, and she could not stop crying. She was hungover and emotional and had made a decision that was completely out of character. It went against her values and goals and made her terribly unhappy for years afterward. I know that a barn wasn't where she wanted to have one of the most pivotal experiences of her life. This is what happens when teens put alcohol into the mix.

The lockstep march of alcohol and hookup culture is very sad. To make matters worse, I believe alcohol and hookups have created a double bind for young people. Alcohol has a terrific dopamine reward when it is consumed.[28] Needless to say, sex is also a great dopamine producer. The double bind is that sex and alcohol work in concert to produce alcohol abuse or dependency in millions of college students nationwide. Using the criteria in the *DSM-5*, short for the *Diagnostic and Statistical Manual of Mental Disorders 5*, we learn that 40 percent of college students have mild to severe alcohol-use disorder.[29]

Among the many disturbing things about hookup culture is the degree to which young women feel conflicted about it.

ULTIMATELY DISSATISFYING

One research study, involving some thirty-three hundred adults aged seventeen to forty, reported that 54 percent of women had overall negative feelings about having one-night stands.[30] In another study of six hundred college students, women were twice as likely to report having feelings of regret after a hookup than men.[31] It is clear from the research findings that regret and hookup sex go hand in hand. Yet, like moths to a flame, many young women are drawn to hooking up.

Why the disconnect? I suspect it has a lot to do with the pressure to conform. If your peer group is hooking up, you want to belong. One student said, "If you're not doing it, then you're the odd one out and everyone sees you in a different way." Another said, "It seems like everyone is doing it … so that is why a lot of girls may feel trapped."

I think that girls who are dissatisfied with hookups feel that way because deep down they want something more. A sixteen-year-old girl wrote this about hookups: "I was hooking up with a boy, but not having sex with him. At first, I was fine with hooking up. We were getting something we both wanted, so that was fine. But because I liked his personality, I started to develop deeper feelings for him. After a little bit, after we hooked up, I would feel [terrible], and I realized this was because of these deeper feelings that were not being met by a hookup."

No matter how a girl acts or how much she may say she wants to have sex like a man, she is still a woman. In a survey of college-age women, 83 percent admitted they wanted "a traditional romantic relationship as opposed to an uncommitted sexual relationship."[32] Additionally, recent research indicates casual sex is linked to higher rates of depression, loneliness, and guilt.[33] No wonder hookup culture leaves girls dissatisfied.

For a girl who believes sex comes without consequences, nothing could be more dangerous than hookup culture. The lie of hookup culture says it is okay to have friends with benefits. Hookup culture says it is just fine to be sexually intimate with someone you barely know. One student said, "If you aren't getting hit on by a guy or haven't hooked up with one in a while, a girl's confidence will lower and instead of asking what is wrong about the hookup culture itself, she'll wonder what is wrong with her."

Too many girls are paying the price for not questioning hookup culture. Perhaps returning to some old-fashioned advice could eliminate that cost.

GRANDMA WAS RIGHT

My grandma Myrtle had some old-fashioned ideas. She called African Americans "black people" and sometimes even "Negroes." What can you expect from someone born in 1912? She cleaned her windows with vinegar. She insisted on using old T-shirts as rags. My grandma thought butterfly art—you know, crystals, stickers, and mobiles featuring the winged creatures—was high culture. She thought my various hairstyles throughout my teenage years were, and I quote, "ridiculous." But she was right about one thing: you shouldn't sleep around. And she didn't need a social scientist to tell her she was right. But one did.

One significant study in 2011 proved my grandma Myrtle right. Though many previous studies had shown a correlation between premarital sex and divorce rates, none had sought to identify a causal relationship between adolescent sex and marital dissolution. In this study a nationally representative sample of 7,643 women was interviewed. Among other things, they were asked about their age the first time they had sexual intercourse and whether they "really wanted," "had mixed feelings," or "really didn't want" it.

The results of this groundbreaking study were significant. The first finding was that when a girl has sex before the age of sixteen, wanted or not, this has a *causal* relationship to higher divorce rates later in life. In the words of the study, "first intercourse during adolescence may change attitudes and beliefs about marriage and sex—such as the permanency of marriage." Something about early sexual experiences changes a girl's mind-set and makes her more likely to divorce. Clearly, sex is not just sex. It is something more.

A second significant finding is that girls of any age who did not completely want their first sexual experience are at higher risk of marital dissolution. The relationship between unwanted sex and divorce is a causal one and not explained by other factors. The study confirms what all women know: the first time matters. This causes me to think some serious thoughts about divorce rates in the future, as many girls are now losing their virginity in hookups when that is not really what they want.

The final two findings of note are related to each other. First, this study concludes "premarital sexual outcomes all increase the risk of marital dissolution." My takeaway from that finding is that the more sexual encounters and sexual partners, the greater the risk of divorce. The second finding was that women who marry as virgins have lower marital dissolution rates.[34] In brief, the age at which a girl first has sex and the number of sexual partners she has had both have a direct impact on her prospects for a lifelong marriage. Somewhere my grandma is saying, "I told you so."

PREPARING YOUR DAUGHTER FOR FUTURE HAPPINESS
KNOW WHAT IS HAPPENING IN HER LIFE

When I interviewed young women about the high school hookup culture, I also asked them, "What do you think parents should know about hookup culture?" All of them agreed that "parents need to know that it happens."

One girl said, "Just because your daughter is not in a relationship does not mean she is not having sex." Each of the high school students said that parents are largely clueless that hookups are even happening. It is not just a college phenomenon; it is a high school one too.

Another student said, "Parents need to understand that hookups can happen anywhere." I heard from all of the women I spoke with that parents should be open and willing to talk about hookup culture, even if it makes us uncomfortable. If we want to help our daughters avoid disaster, we cannot be naive about this reality. We need to know what is happening in their lives.

This means talking to your daughter and asking her many questions. When Jacquelyn was in high school and dating secretly, her mother and I did not ask the right questions. As our daughters have gotten older, we have become better at this. Asking questions is a tough but necessary part of parenting. In our family my wife plays this role with our girls. I spend a great deal of time with my daughters and talk to them more than most fathers. But there is something different about how my wife is able to talk with them. She gets them to share and talk openly about things in a way that would be impossible for me.

Part of being alert is also knowing what is happening in your daughter's digital life. Though our family did not have hard-and-fast rules about technology, Tamara and I stayed involved in our children's digital lives. All parents have to decide how much they will monitor electronic communication. I don't think parents in this day and age can afford to go "ostrich" and put their heads in the sand when it comes to the digital life of their daughters. I believe you should monitor your daughter's Facebook page, cell phone, and social media apps. Until she is mature, she needs to know you will protect her from herself when it comes to social media.

Jacquelyn:

Even though you aren't supposed to, I use the same password for just about everything. I wish that my parents would have known my password and been able to monitor my use of technology when I was a teen.

Your daughter has even more access to communication than I ever did. I think that it is perfectly fine for you to have her passwords and log into her social media—but let her know you are doing so. This will help hold her accountable and also provide her with a hedge of protection in the very scary Internet age. Think of it as a firewall for her heart and her future. Anything that she posts online is available to anyone anytime. I would also advocate for not letting her have Snapchat at all. The premise is that the pictures "go away" once you send them. I bet you can imagine what that is used for ...

Even with open lines of communication, parents still have to look beyond the words of their children and into other areas of their lives. As parents we want to assume the best, but always be alert for the worst. For example, you should be concerned that your daughter may be hooking up if:

- She is going to parties or coed sleepovers. (People aren't playing pin the tail on the donkey. Sorry, times have changed.)
- She spends a lot of time with one boy alone, but he is not her "boyfriend."
- She is constantly communicating with one boy in particular, but he is not her "boyfriend."
- She is "just talking" to said boy.
- She is talking to this boy but doesn't spend any time with him in a group setting or she doesn't know any of his friends.

TEACH HER THE LONG-TERM CONSEQUENCES OF TEEN SEX

1. She will be hurt emotionally from premarital sex.
2. The earlier she begins to have sex and the more sex partners she has, the greater the likelihood she will end up divorced.

Jacquelyn:
Sometimes I would be watching TV or just spending time with my parents and they would seize the moment and talk

with me and my siblings about sex, divorce, and a variety of issues. These conversations are some of the most cherished of my childhood. They would turn off the TV, face me, and engage in my life. How awesome! It made these conversations feel natural, and less like my parents were preaching to us. While I didn't always take the messages to heart, I have not forgotten them and they help me sometimes even today.

EMPHASIZE OVER AND OVER THE LINK BETWEEN ALCOHOL AND SEX

I would make sure my daughter understood clearly that boys and girls metabolize alcohol differently. The fact is girls get drunker with less alcohol and stay drunk longer.[35] One of the dangers of teen drinking is that girls don't recognize their own limits and often end up in dangerous situations because they are far more inebriated than they realize.

I would also let my daughter know that unwanted sex and alcohol use go hand in hand. There is plenty of research on the topic you could show her. And it is ever present in the media. The next time you see a relevant news article, blog post, or TV piece, I would take note of it and share it with your daughter.

Jacquelyn:

If at all possible, never, ever, ever let your daughter be in a place where drinking and sex could conceivably happen. In our family, we talk about the "hedge of protection" that parents provide their children. Sometimes I would get mad that my parents wouldn't let me go somewhere as a teen, but looking back, I'm really glad they set boundaries like this. You cannot block 100 percent of your daughter's opportunities to make mistakes, but you can limit the number of times she is exposed to these negative experiences.

WATCH THE PBS FRONTLINE EPISODE "INSIDE THE TEENAGE BRAIN"

Watch the episode mentioned above with your daughter. It will give you both remarkable insight into how the teenage brain works and how behaviors of the teenage years can be imprinted on the brain. It should be a great starting place for a discussion on which behaviors she is already hardwiring into her brain circuitry.

MAKE SURE SHE KNOWS IT'S NEVER TOO LATE TO START AGAIN

If you are the parent of a daughter who has made some mistakes, there is good news for her.

Jacquelyn:
We all make mistakes. Teenagers make disproportionately more of these mistakes than adults. I look back on my teenage years and wonder how I even made it out alive and whole! I made some really, really awful choices, but I came out the other side. I might have learned a few lessons the hard way, but that doesn't mean I was broken by my experiences. I have a master's degree and am living out my calling

as a high school teacher. I have great friends and a wonderful, full life. This can be your daughter's future too. We are created to be resilient, to come through challenges on the other side, but your daughter needs your guidance on this journey. I still talk to my mom about four times a day!

The good news is that your daughter's future is not etched in stone. The Bible speaks about being "changed from the inside out."[36] Another version says "be transformed by the renewing of your mind."[37] Though I'm not a Bible scholar, I think what is being said is that we are capable of thinking and acting differently, no matter what has happened in the past. Young people have brain plasticity, which allows them to learn and change and develop new neural circuitry. I believe the damage of premarital sex may be undone with a commitment to an old-fashioned standard of sexuality. It is possible for a girl to start over. The more we can encourage and help our daughters embrace a traditional approach to sexuality, the more likely they are to be happy in the future.[38]

QUESTIONS FOR REFLECTION

1. How can you make your daughter comfortable when discussing difficult topics?
2. How are you protecting your daughter from being involved in hookups?
3. How have you communicated to your daughter that having sex today has an impact on her marriage and future happiness? In what ways does she know this to be true?

4. Does your approach to drinking give tacit permission to your daughter to drink? What message is being communicated to your daughter about the use of alcohol?

QUESTIONS FOR YOU AND YOUR DAUGHTER TO DISCUSS

1. How do you believe sex will help you stay married in the future? How will premarital sex affect this?
2. Can you think of another trusted adult with whom you can talk about sex as well?
3. Why do the people you know hook up?

LOOKING AHEAD TO THE NEXT CHAPTER

Not every girl will experience all of the dating myths in this book. But one thing is 98 percent certain. If your daughter has a boyfriend in high school, they will break up. And when they do, if they have been sexually active, she may be tempted to fall under the spell of dating myth #7: *It is okay to break up and get back together.*

It's Okay to Break Up and Get Back Together

As I approached a hipster café in southeast Portland, I was nervous. I had arranged to meet a former student to discuss her tumultuous three-year relationship with her boyfriend and wasn't sure what to expect. I had known Serena for a number of years and found her to be a sensitive and insightful young woman, but I was uncertain about the possibility of a dramatic, tear-filled scene. We sat together and shared some small talk and ordered breakfast.

Over the next hour I gained a look into the thoughts and emotions of a young woman who believes it is okay to break up and get back together. By her own account, Serena said she and Billy broke up and got back together six times during their three-year relationship, which spanned her senior year of high school through her second year of college. Her words will pepper the pages of this chapter and are testimony to both her pain and her resilience.

I believe adults in general underestimate the toxicity of on-again, off-again relationships. As one who has seen them close up, I believe any scenario in which your teenage daughter breaks up and gets back together with her boyfriend has the potential to be extremely harmful to her. I hope this chapter will give you some insight and tools to guide your daughter through a breakup.

WHY COUPLES BREAK UP AND GET BACK TOGETHER, OVER AND OVER
OUCH! IT HURTS

Most of us have experienced the heartbreak of romantic rejection. It is nearly universal. And when it happens, it hurts. A lot. (Even when you know it is the right thing to do!) Why? Because emotional pain and physical pain feel much alike. In fact, a study by researchers at Columbia University confirmed that physical pain and emotional pain are both at work after a romantic breakup. After showing recently jilted partners a picture of their ex and asking them to think about being rejected, the researchers scanned the participants' brains using functional MRI. They discovered that the parts of the brain that process physical pain were active in this scenario.[1] From the brain's vantage, a relationship ending causes physical pain.

Other biological factors are also at work during a breakup. First, there is a long-term drop in neurochemicals that were flush while the relationship was ongoing. The pleasure of dopamine and oxytocin that a person enjoyed from physical and emotional intimacy is now in retreat. The feelings of euphoria and bliss she was experiencing with young love have been suddenly replaced by loneliness. Serena said that after she and her boyfriend broke up, "I cried for like two days straight. You feel like a broken woman when a relationship ends."

A breakup brings a rise in cortisol,[2] the hormone our bodies produce when we are under stress. Elevated levels of cortisol are responsible for the uncomfortable sensations of stress. As part of the "fight or flight response," the hormone elevates heart rate, accelerates breathing, and impairs cognition. Long-term elevated levels of cortisol are linked to suppressed functioning in the following areas: immune system, digestion, reproductive capabilities, and sleep patterns.

This increase in cortisol likely contributes to many of the problems that people encounter when a relationship ends: poor concentration, inability to sleep, and loss of appetite are all part of our body's response to stress.[3] An ending relationship produces a potent mix of physical pain, emotional distress, falling hormone levels, and a cortisol-flooded body, which taken together make a girl who has just ended a relationship wholly miserable. The question is, how will she respond to this crisis?

"I WANT A NEW DRUG"

A girl who has just experienced a breakup can respond in a number of ways. The first is what psychiatrists call *abandonment rage*. Many times over the years I've listened to a girl vent, yell, and rage over a breakup. Usually either the boy broke up with her out of the blue or she dumped him because he was cheating. The level of anger can be intense. But out of this anger comes a righteous indignation that helps her move on. While the breakup hurts, she quickly accepts the realization that she is better off without him. When this happens, there is a "clean" break that doesn't allow her to believe that getting back together with her boyfriend is okay.

If my daughter were experiencing abandonment rage, I would let the process play out and take hold. I would be a good listener to help her move on. If her rage subsided and she began to think about getting back together with the boy, I would put together a plan for how to support her and to diminish the discomfort and pain that the breakup had caused her to feel. (I will talk more about how to do this later in the chapter.)

Some girls don't experience abandonment rage but instead enter into what psychiatrists call the *protest stage*. Sometimes a girl who has just been through a breakup will act like an addict in need of a fix. In the 1980s Huey Lewis and the News sang "I Want a New Drug." Some girls need a new drug. As Serena put it, "Billy wanted me, and I liked that. And that was the drug. Being wanted." But the problem is the new drug is the old drug. In my experience this response is most common when the relationship that has ended has been an extended one. A girl in the protest stage wants to get her reward system back in place. And the reward system is based on one person only—her ex.

If she was dumped, she may obsess with getting back together with him. This fixation may take many forms. She may try to bump into him somewhere in hopes of reconciling. She may subtweet about him. This is where a girl may tweet "I'm so hurting right now" in hopes that her tweet will get retweeted back to her boyfriend, prompting reconciliation. She may even text the boy directly in the hopes of getting back together. I saw this most recently in the case of a boy in one of my classes. I was talking with him and he kept getting text messages. I knew he had been dating a girl, so I jokingly said, "Your girlfriend won't stop texting you!" He responded, "We broke up a week ago and she won't stop texting me." (Many months later I would bail this young man out of jail after a verbal altercation with this same girl!) I see this type of behavior all the time from girls who have been jilted.

Jacquelyn:

I am guilty of this! I can remember once asking my ex-boyfriend for a list of all the things I needed to fix in order to get back together with him. I was like a woman possessed. This breakup had me practically groveling.

If the girl dumps the boy, she will go back to him and say it was a big mistake and seek reconciliation. Far too many girls go crawling back when they should be walking—or should I say running—away. Serena told me, "After the first time we broke up, we got back together and he got on his knees and told me he loved me and wanted to marry me. When a guy tells you all that stuff ... you know ... he was my first boyfriend. It was so great and he was so romantic."

SHE GOT BACK TOGETHER WITH HIM; NOW WHAT?

Once the relationship is rekindled, things between the couple will be better, but only for a while. Serena gives a textbook example: "It was always happy go lucky for three months. He was nice and said all the nice things he always did." But if you recall from dating myth #1, the process of hedonic adaptation is always at work. Hedonic adaptation is the principle that pleasurable things become less pleasurable over time. A rekindled relationship is no exception. The flood of emotions in the restored relationship will eventually dry up, and a couple will soon be right back where they were before the breakup. The same unresolved issues that prompted the breakup are still right there, front and center.

When the novelty of the "new" relationship has worn off, a couple will usually break up again. Typically everyone learns their lesson and the couple splits for good. But a small number of couples can't seem to learn the lesson, and they start the cycle all over again. Break up, protest, get back together, adaptation, misery, break up, protest, get back together, adaptation, misery, break up, protest, get back together … ad nauseam. Just like the directions on the back of the shampoo bottle: lather, rinse, repeat. (Who really does that?)

Each time she breaks up, a girl finds herself back at square one—in this case dating myth #1: If I had a boyfriend I would be happy. She is now likely to cycle through each of the myths again. Once she is back with her boyfriend, she trusts her feelings (dating myth #2), and she believes that she is in love (dating myth #3) and that sex will enhance their relationship (dating myth #4). Soon she convinces herself that love and sex are the same (dating myth #5) and that sex comes without consequences (dating myth #6). All the while she lives out dating myth #7: It's okay to break up and get back together. A girl who is in this lather, rinse, repeat cycle progresses through each of the myths again and again. It's as if she is Bill Murray's character in the movie *Groundhog Day*, only there is no magical moment when she will live happily ever after.

Every high school has this couple. During my second year of teaching, Josh and Hilary were that couple. Everybody knew them. Their fights were volcanic and legendary. Their breakups were the stuff of Hollywood production. Proclamations of disgust and utterances of the word *never* were common. In those few moments of lucidity after a breakup, Hilary would say things like "I am so stupid.

Why did I get back together with him?" But in due time this couple always got back together.

Jacquelyn:

If you ask your daughter, she will know a couple just like this. They yell at each other in the hallway, they skip classes just to argue, and they are definitely breaking up and getting back together. At my high school, our version of this couple was a particularly spectacular failure. I asked my friend (who was in this volatile relationship) if she knew how many times she and her boyfriend had broken up and gotten back together. Even she didn't know, but she estimated it to be over twenty times. They broke up in person, on the phone, in text messages. They got back together at lunch, during class, and after school. There were many times when I heard her say that he was "disgusting," "awful," "the worst boyfriend ever." Twenty minutes later, they would be holding hands and walking down the hallway. Neither one had a life to return to after a breakup, so they went back to the only place they could—a deeply flawed relationship. It was sad to see them walking down the halls, holding hands, staring ahead with a thousand-mile stare.

The most dangerous part of this misery is the dependency it brings. Serena told me, "If he didn't answer my texts, I thought I had done or said something wrong. If he didn't hang out with me, I felt like he didn't like me anymore. I just needed his attention all the time." When a girl is trapped in the on-again, off-again relationship, it fosters a dangerous dependency. In the best of circumstances this dependency weakens a young woman and robs her of her value as she begins to define herself by the status of the relationship. (Serena: "I constantly craved his acceptance and his wanting of me.") She is good if the relationship is good, and she is bad if the relationship is bad. (Serena: "If Billy was not happy with me, I would think, *I'm a horrible person*. He made it so that I was always just wanting to please him, because if I wasn't pleasing him, he would be angry with me. All of our arguments were me doing something wrong that he didn't like and I would have to change that. I would have to beg him to stay with me.") When a girl is emotionally beaten down and believes she is worthless, she will accept the harshest treatment from her boyfriend. As we will see in the next chapter, in the worst of circumstances this dependency can leave her vulnerable to manipulation and abuse.

THE ULTIMATE REASON BREAKING UP IS HARD TO DO

In the Hebrew Scriptures the word for sex is *echad*. It literally means "one." I talked with a rabbi friend of mine about this word, and he explained that in Scripture God said that "they shall become one [*echad*] flesh."[4] He explained to me that making love is "the holiest thing a man and woman can do in marriage."[5] In other words, *echad* is much more than what we think of as the act of sex. It goes much deeper. Being one has emotional, intellectual, and spiritual dimensions that transcend the physical. According to this rabbi, *echad* is "opening up a secret part of yourself and sharing it with the person." In his book *Loveology*, John Mark Comer framed it this way: when a couple is having sex, they are connected "at a primal level that's hard to break."[6]

I believe this primal connection, or *echad*, is what makes it so hard for a girl to extricate herself from an on-again, off-again relationship. We are meant to be connected at a much deeper level. We yearn for this all-encompassing connection that is "primal," that is *echad*. (This is part of the reason that hookup sex is damaging as well. Even in a "low investment" hookup there is often the hope for something more—a longing for a deep connection. This may be part of the reason hookup sex leaves girls largely dissatisfied.) In the on-again, off-again relationship sex binds a couple together and makes it very hard for them to stay apart. For Serena and Billy, "sex was probably the only affection I could get from him. He'd be superaffectionate in the beginning, but he would get distant toward the end of each of our relationships. Sex was the only 'he loves me' time I could get."

For young and immature couples, the sex—and the desire for so much more—is what holds the relationship together in the first place. I'm not sure I've ever encountered any dysfunctional on-again, off-again relationship that wasn't in large part held together by sex. Oftentimes a girl who has ended a relationship is drawn back into the orbit of her ex because what she really wants is that connection and to rekindle the relationship. This was certainly true for Serena. She had this to say about how she got back together with Billy after one of their breakups: "We were trying to be civil and talking to each other. One night I stayed a little bit late at his house and we ended up sleeping together. And that is how we got back together. He did the whole 'I really do love you and let's get back together' thing. Sex was a segue into getting back together. Sex was a segue into 'Wow! We really do love each other.' But it was just sex."

It is not uncommon for a boy to use sex to his advantage. When I was young, we called this "stage II" of a breakup. Stage I was breaking up, and stage II was what you did when you had a hard time breaking up: still having sex even though you were no longer dating. One girl describes how she got sucked into this very thing:

> In my sophomore and junior years of high school I dated this "amazing" guy for a little over a year and then right out of nowhere he broke up with me and broke my heart. My cousin gave me the advice not to talk to my ex. She told me every time he tried to contact me to ignore him. Sadly, I didn't listen.
>
> He called me about a week after I got this advice. He asked me if I wanted to come over to his house and talk. All I wanted was to be with him again, so I got in my car and sped over to his house. When I got there he started telling me that he was so lonely and that he wanted to have a friend with benefits, and then he asked me if I wanted to be that girl. I excitedly jumped at the chance.
>
> I thought if we started having sex again, like we used to when we dated, he would want me back. We were having sex for the next month. We would get together and then I would want to talk to him all the time, but after he got what he wanted, he

wouldn't talk to me until he wanted sex again. Once I realized that I was being used I felt horrible about myself. The pain was easily worse than what I had felt after we broke up.

Unfortunately, this scenario is all too common. Sadly, the great longing for *echad* can bind people together in ways that just aren't good.

Serena made a final break with Billy only after she rebuilt the life she had sacrificed during her years with him. She said, "When I came to college, I was lucky enough to make friends. I found my community. When Billy and I got back together for the final time, I tried to keep my friends and do other things besides being his girlfriend because I wasn't happy just being his girlfriend. I decided I needed to be a person outside my relationship with him. It was the smartest thing I did, because if I had just done 'I'm Billy's girlfriend' in my social life, then when we again broke up I would have been in the same boat as before and gotten back together with him. I've been able to stay away from Billy by investing in my own life and doing me. I'm doing so many things now. I just invested more time in myself." At the time she told me this, Serena had been single for over three years. I know she will not go back to him.

WHAT'S AT STAKE?

Some parents may look at teenage dating and think breaking up and getting back together are harmless and cute. After all, this behavior happens as early as middle school and no one seems to be harmed by it. You may think it is just part of the maturing process that a girl goes through as she dates. But I believe much more is at stake. What is the learned relationship behavior that she will take into marriage? If the on-again, off-again relationship becomes a girl's modus operandi, it is unlikely she will be able to be a steady and reliable partner in marriage. That's why it is so critical that you help your daughter avoid breaking up and getting back together.

PREPARING YOUR DAUGHTER FOR FUTURE HAPPINESS

After they have gone through a breakup, I always tell my students that they are very likely not going to marry the other person and ask them why they would get back together only to break up later, as it seems like a dramatic waste of time. As parents we need to help our daughters through a breakup so they won't be trapped in the on-again, off-again cycle.

I believe the first step toward protecting our daughters from this cycle is a practical and proactive one.

SET SOME LIMITS WELL BEFORE SHE STARTS DATING

Do what you can to encourage your daughter to have a life outside of her boyfriend. To me this means setting some limits on the amount of time she can spend with him and the frequency they see and communicate with each other. This can be difficult because in a texting, tweeting, Instagramming, and Snapchatting world, there are so many opportunities for a couple to stay engaged with each other—even when they are apart.

Jacquelyn:
As I mentioned earlier, a one-to-one ratio is a healthy balance when it comes to balancing friendships and boyfriend. This can be a hard balance for anyone, particularly a young woman. In high school I remember watching a certain couple's friends slowly dwindle down to two. When they first started dating, this couple sat at a cafeteria table that was full with their group of friends. Every month or so, one of their friends would move to a different place to eat lunch. Soon, the couple was eating lunch by themselves. The balance in their relationships was all wrong.

For every one hour your daughter spends with her boyfriend, she should probably spend one hour with a friend or close family member. For every one text she sends to her boyfriend, it is healthy for her to send one text to someone else. If this ratio seems disproportionate, I would say that this is a cause for concern. Take it from me; you never want your daughter isolated by her relationship. Encourage and enforce the one-to-one ratio with her.

One way our family has managed this problem is that when we are together in the car, or at a movie, or over dinner, no one is allowed to text. I've said to my own children many times that the people you are with at that very moment are valuable and deserve your full attention. Another family I know has their kids turn over their smartphones to their parents at bedtime. So many young people text, tweet, and look at their phones late into the night that I believe this is a good practice—even if your children are not dating.

Jacquelyn:

It is okay to insist that your daughter's phone be outside her bedroom at night. In fact, I think that is a wise policy. If I had had the technology girls have today, I would have gotten into a lot more trouble behind closed doors.

I recommend that you consider the following questions when deciding what limits to set for your daughter:

- How many texts to her boyfriend should your daughter be sending during homework time? What about during meals?
- What time should she be off her phone in the evening?
- How much time should she spend talking on the phone with her boyfriend each day?
- If she and her boyfriend spent the day together at school, how often should they be hanging out on school nights?
- How many different mediums does she have to communicate with her boyfriend? How many is too many?

Every family will have to muddle through this issue because there isn't a one-size-fits-all answer. But I do know this: when a couple has unfettered connectedness, their world can get mighty small, mighty fast.

HAVE AN ACTION PLAN

I've heard it said, "When you fail to plan, you plan to fail." Nothing could be truer for a breakup. Just ask Serena. When she and Billy would break up, she had no plan to avoid getting back together with him. Because her world was very small, the connection she had to her boyfriend was intense and difficult to break. Serena said, "We always got back together in the summers because I got bored. I would stalk his Facebook page and Twitter feed because I was obsessed with him. I would stay up late at night and I would send him texts. I didn't have a lot of friends or anybody I could hang out with. So it was like 'What else am I going to do?' So I had all this time and started hanging out with him."

If your daughter is in a serious dating relationship, I urge you to have a plan in place *before* the breakup about how you will keep her busy after the breakup. Your daughter will be most vulnerable in the early days and weeks after the relationship ends. Whatever this plan is, it should involve lots of Kleenex, chocolate, and money. Yes, I said money. Take her to the movies, out shopping, out to dinner, and maybe even on a weekend excursion. Whatever your plan looks like, the goal is singular—to help your daughter not go crawling back to her ex.

Jacquelyn:
Based on my experience, I recommend that your plan include things like the following:

- *A change of scenery.* Be ready to whisk your daughter away to another location. In the immediate day or so after the breakup, get your daughter as far removed from her usual setting as possible. What about a weekend trip? What about her friend's house on the other side of town? What about bowling? Anything is a good distraction.

- *Companionship.* Don't let her spend much time alone. Surround her with supportive, loving, entertaining people who aren't her boyfriend. Invite over a beloved aunt, her friends, her grandma. Anyone who will be both a listening ear as well as a welcome distraction.

- *Communication monitoring.* Limit contact with her ex as much as possible. Part of bouncing back from a split ought to be reinvesting in yourself and in relationships with other people. The less she talks to her ex, the better she will be able to move through this breakup and come out the other side stronger. Encourage her to delete him from her phone, Instagram, and Facebook. It is all too easy for her to reconnect with her ex in the virtual world. The more barriers between her and the ex, the more likely she will move on and process the experience.

- *An at-school plan.* If your daughter goes to school with her boyfriend, help her craft a plan to avoid said boyfriend at school. Does she have a friend who can help her? I would suggest the buddy system with a particularly bold girlfriend. Let your daughter's other relationships act as a cushion for her at school during this recovery period.

• *Parent-to-parent communication.* If your daughter is under sixteen, you might call the parents of the ex-boyfriend. While you might have a great plan in place, they might not. Try to get both families to agree to keep the couple separate in every possible way for the time being. If her ex is constantly trying to communicate with your daughter, it will be much harder for her to hold the line and stay broken up with him.

• *A new dopamine and oxytocin replacement.* Your daughter has been getting all sorts of happy feelings from her boyfriend. These feelings now need to come from other places, including lots of regular hugs from Mom and Dad.

BE ON HER TEAM

When your daughter breaks up with her boyfriend, he is *dead to you*. Seriously. *Dead. To. You.* That means you must stop all contact with him. A parent can inadvertently push a couple back together by maintaining communication with the ex. Your daughter needs to know that you are behind her, giving her the strength to stand up for herself even when she doesn't have the strength for herself.

We all make mistakes. Teenagers make disproportionately more of these mistakes than adults. Try to remember your own failings and struggles when you talk to your daughter in the aftermath of a breakup. This might be the best time for you to work on building a connection with her.

APPLY WET LOGIC TO AN EMOTIONAL FIRE

What if your daughter is weak and wants to go back to her ex? One strategy would be to apply wet logic to an emotional fire. If she broke up with him, help her focus on the reasons why. Remember, she will be looking back at her relationship with rose-colored glasses. She will need to be reminded of why she dumped him. If she was dumped, she needs to be made strong in her weakness.

I think it is important for a girl in this situation to be told that her ex intentionally hurt her. He thought about breaking up with her. He formulated a plan and rehearsed a lame speech that probably involved the words "we can still be friends." He took her heart in his hand and smashed it with his fist. Remind your daughter that she is valuable. Teach her that when a boy hurts her, she does not go back to that boy. She does not beg to get a boy back who caused her pain. A girl who will take a boy back when he hurts her heart may take him back when he breaks her bones too.

DON'T MAKE A POWER PLAY

Even with all your planning and reasoning, your daughter may still want to get back together with an ex. So what do you do then?

Whatever you do, don't make a power play against your teen daughter—unless the relationship holds the threat of harm for her.

If you cannot convince your daughter to refrain from getting back together with her ex, you might try this approach: have her talk to an older sibling, aunt, or trusted adult about the situation. You may not be able to help her see clearly, but someone else might. For twenty-three years I've been saying the same things to students that their parents have been saying to them. I can't tell you how many times my students have said to me, "That is exactly what my parents said. But somehow it makes more sense when I hear it from you." Hopefully you have another adult whom your child can go to for advice. The more resources at her disposal, the safer she will be. But ultimately you are the frontline defense for your daughter. Your ability to help her develop healthy dating habits after a breakup will benefit her for her entire lifetime.

QUESTIONS FOR REFLECTION

1. Do you have any valuable lessons you learned from a breakup? What did you learn that you can pass on to your daughter?
2. If your daughter broke up tomorrow with her boyfriend, what would your breakup plan look like?
3. How would you explain to your daughter that sex fuses two people together?

QUESTIONS FOR YOU AND YOUR DAUGHTER TO DISCUSS

1. Why is getting back together with an ex-boyfriend a bad idea?

2. What reasons might a girl have for going back to an ex-boyfriend?

3. Why would a girl break up with her boyfriend and still hook up with him? How might this be dangerous?

4. Do you know anybody who is in a break-up-and-get-back-together relationship? In what ways do they seem like unhealthy people?

LOOKING AHEAD TO THE NEXT CHAPTER

Thankfully the break-up-and-get-back-together relationship is the exception and not the rule. But for a girl mired in this relationship, there are additional dangers as well. Sometimes these relationships can turn very ugly. When this happens, a girl will believe dating myth #8: *He will never hit me again.*

Dating Myth #8

He Will Never Hit Me Again

Don't read one more word before you answer this question: What percentage of high school students report being physically hurt, slapped, or hit in a dating relationship? It is more common than most of us think. One estimate is that 81 percent of parents don't believe dating violence is an issue for their teen or say they do not know if it is an issue.[1] Yet, according to the Centers for Disease Control and Prevention, approximately 1.5 million high school students are victims of physical abuse by a dating partner. Nearly a third of adolescents are victims of sexual, physical, emotional, and/ or verbal abuse from a dating partner. And almost 10 percent of high school students report being physically hurt, slapped, or hit in a dating relationship.[2]

Regardless of the exact numbers, one thing is abundantly clear: far too many of our teen daughters are the victims of dating violence. And for some of you reading this chapter, it could literally be life and death for your daughter. This chapter examines some warning signs of potential abuse that you can share with your daughter and offers you resources for talking to your daughter about a topic adults don't talk about enough.

WHY RELATIONSHIPS BECOME VIOLENT
HIGH EMOTIONAL STRESS AND POOR IMPULSE CONTROL

In researching for this chapter, I interviewed Christine Ourada, the director of a woman's recovery program in Portland, Oregon, that deals with the deep effects of abuse and domestic violence.[3] She agrees that pattern is a part of abusive relationships: "Breaking up and getting back together is the dominant relationship pattern we see." The very nature of the on-again, off-again relationship lends itself to emotional stress, which can trigger abuse in some males.

When an unhealthy relationship is not allowed to die a natural death, each new argument takes on extraordinary importance. The on-again, off-again relationship fails to end over conflicts about concerns such as cheating, jealousy, controlling behavior, violence, and more. Very serious flaws in people are ignored for the sake of keeping the relationship intact. When two people who are an ill fit ignore substantial problems in each other or in their relationship, they find themselves in a pressure cooker.

This pressure is often the result of what I call a too-much, too-soon (TMTS) relationship in which a couple acts as though their relationship is permanent even though it probably has no chance of being permanent. They spend incredible amounts of time together—at school, after school, weekends, evenings, and more. This time together extends into the world of technology, which enables them to be in touch even when they are apart. They are connected via text, Skype, Facebook, Instagram, Snapchat, and many other communication platforms. As we've discussed, this time together is often at the expense of other significant relationships and activities.

Girls in TMTS relationships share their entire life stories with their boyfriends after knowing them only a few weeks. Couples in TMTS relationships often become significant emotional supports for each other. I think it is wonderful that teens want to support each other, but this emotional support can look a great deal like married couples leaning on each other in tough times. Not too long ago I was talking with a young girl who for six months had been dating a boy who had drug and family problems. In her words, she was "trying to help him." This kind of attitude is typical of girls in TMTS relationships. She had overinvested emotionally in her boyfriend to the point that she was taking on his emotional burdens. That is an adult behavior. Most teens aren't ready for that kind of commitment.

TMTS relationships, in the end, are artificial. By that I mean they are poor copies of the relationships of mature and healthy adults. (By the way, adults can get into TMTS relationships too!) The level of emotional investment, time spent, sacrifice, and physical involvement is out of balance with the teen's emotional maturity and critical-thinking skills. Though dating violence is most common in break-up-and-get-back-together relationships, it can occur when dating teens take on adult problems without the benefit of mature, adult brains.

When teens are immersed in too-much, too-soon relationships, they begin to tackle adult problems. This is particularly true if they are spending a great deal of time together, acting like a married couple, and taking on issues they shouldn't be taking on. For example, if a teenage boy cheats on a teenage girl, she should end the relationship immediately. They are not married. There are no children to consider. No lifetime commitment to take into account. End of story. However, I've seen teens stay together after one of them has cheated. It is hard enough for married couples to take on this problem, let alone teens who are still maturing. Their brains are still developing, and the last areas of the brain to develop are those that regulate impulse control.[4] When teens try to discuss a complicated issue like cheating without the benefit of fully developed impulse control, the results can be violent.

I tell high school students all the time about the Taco Bell or McDonald's rule, which is this: if a couple is arguing about something more serious than whether to eat at Taco Bell or McDonald's, then both need to ditch the relationship. Any argument more serious than this is an indicator of a poor relationship, particularly if the arguments are repeated. I tell them, "High school should be some of the best and most carefree times of your life. Do not ruin it by maintaining an unhealthy, high-stress relationship."

Jacquelyn:

When I was in high school, I was in an unhealthy, high-stress relationship and knew other girls in the same predicament. The following list describes some of the behavioral changes a girl can make as a result of the emotional stress she is under.

- Stress indicators: losing weight, lack of sleep, irritability.
- Her other relationships may begin to break down, particularly her friendships.
- She experiences some core changes in who she once was, that is, starts acting ditzy or dressing differently, begins listening to different types of music.

- She becomes overly self-critical: your once-confident daughter seems to lose her sense of confidence or self.
- Her friends either don't know that she is in a relationship or really don't like her boyfriend.

Why would a teenage girl stay in an unhealthy, high-stress relationship? I am not an expert in these issues, but I have a lot of experience with teens and have formulated some opinions about this. I believe it is in part because she has abandoned and given up the richness of her life in exchange for being part of a too-much, too-soon relationship. She's left behind friends, interests, and hobbies. As her world becomes smaller, the relationship gets bigger to the point that it defines who she is. Consequently, she believes the relationship must be preserved at all costs. Another reason is that she derives her value and worth from the relationship. When you believe you have no value other than your boyfriend's interest in you, then you'll put up with some serious garbage. Finally, I believe that many abusive relationships are held together by sex. While there is no data on the link between sex and teen dating violence, I suspect this correlation is very strong. When a teen couple is sexually active, the sex leads to many adult emotions and problems confronting immature brains with poor judgment and impulse control. Sex keeps together relationships that should be ending. What is often left is a volatile relationship that shouldn't even exist.

Which brings us to another reason relationships sometimes turn violent.

BOYS AND GIRLS HANDLE STRESS DIFFERENTLY

I have a confession. I don't like to argue with my wife. I will do nearly anything to avoid an argument with her. When I sense an argument coming, I can hardly think straight. When there is a disagreement between us, my heart pounds in my chest and my face gets flushed. When I am under relationship stress, my ears turn bright red and I feel my body tense up. I suspect this feeling is common to many men reading this.

Scientists believe this is part of our "fight or flight" response. The male pathways for stress and aggression are closely aligned with the "fight or flight" response. By and large, men process stress and aggression through the part of the brain that processes physical action.[5] Like most men, my ability to think and communicate is far worse under relational stress. Women, however, are the opposite. Most women communicate better under relational stress. Researchers believe the part of the brain that processes stress and aggression for women is more closely linked to cognitive, emotional, and verbal functions.[6] Unlike boys who process relational stress through physical action, women think more, feel more, and talk more. These gender differences play out in how boys and girls argue.

Because women under stress think, feel, and talk more, they are prone to do what I call the three *c*'s: communicate, cry, and closure. I've watched this scenario play out many times in my classroom at lunchtime. Two girls will come in and say, "Mr. Anderson, can we use your room for a few minutes to talk?" I will say, "Go for it." While I work away at my desk, they communicate with each other. Sometimes there will be moments of heated argument. Sometimes it will be just an intense discussion. There is always a lot of give and take, with each girl listening to the other and often affirming what the other said. After a few minutes of communication, both of them may have a good cry. Tears flow, and they make several trips to my desk for Kleenex. And finally there is closure, complete with a big hug. The girls say things like "You are a great friend, and I can't believe we fought over something so dumb" or "I'm so glad we got this figured out. I don't want anything to ruin our friendship." Some researchers even give this process a name: "tend and befriend."[7] (Not all girls respond to relationship stress so well. But generally girls respond to conflict much better than boys do.)

Boys are just a teensy-weensy bit different when it comes to relationship stress. Because male pathways for stress and aggression run close to the part of their brains that processes physical action, I believe this puts them at a disadvantage when it comes to handling relational stress. While girls communicate, cry, and seek closure to handle a relationship problem, boys do what I like to call the three *s*'s: silent, snap, and strike. I'm of the opinion that most boys can handle about ten minutes of relational stress before they have to be silent and think about the situation. It is as if a boy's ability to think and his ability to talk are mutually exclusive. I'm sure more than one woman reading this is now shouting, "I knew it!"

Problems arise between boys and girls when these two styles clash. When an immature couple gets into an argument, these two styles can be combustible. She wants communication and closure, so she goes to what she does best: words and more words. In her world, conflict is solved through communication and closure. But the problem is, this is not how boys solve crises and handle stress. His first line of defense is silence. He wants to *think* about what is going on, but she wants to *talk* about what is going on. Most boys will quickly grow tired of talking and want to go into their silent space. So they will attempt to put closure on the situation. They might say, "I'm really sorry and I'll try to do better next time." Or, "Yeah, that was really stupid of me. I'll try not to be such a dummy next time." If they are better than the average sixteen-year-old boy, they might even throw in a hug and an "I love you." In a boy's mind, this is good work on his part. Case closed. But in general this is not closure to a girl. She needs more. But he can't give much more.

She thinks, *Maybe I haven't explained myself well enough.* So she tries more words. She searches for the perfect poetic mix of words that will get him to say, "Oh, now I get it. You really want me to do this differently in the future. I see why you feel that way. That was pretty stupid on my part. In the future I'll try harder to make sure I don't do that, because you are really special to me and I would never want this to come between us. I'm so glad you told me about this. I love you so very much and am looking forward to this never happening again. And by the way, you are the greatest thing that has ever happened to me!" Now that is the closure she is looking for. But he cannot give that particular closure. He wants to be silent. So he may try for closure again. "Maybe you didn't hear me. I told you I was sorry." *Now that is closure*, he thinks.

But it is still not closure to her, so she speaks even more words. But he is now in his silent space. He is done talking and listening. It might as well be the Charlie Brown teacher voice he is hearing: "Waa-waaa-wa-waaaa-wa-waaaaa." He has now shut down, so he sits silently while she talks, and talks, and talks, and talks. As she seeks closure, he gets filled with emotions. Soon he is flooded. A man who is flooded will shut down and stonewall, unable to muster any response at all.[8] He is now so stressed out he feels the need to fight with every fiber of his being. This is the point when boys begin to break stuff, punch walls, and maybe even hurt your daughter. Fortunately, most boys choose flight over fight, but some do not.

THOR, GOD OF THE HANDRAIL

I discovered my snapping point a few years ago. Keep in mind that I'm a low-temper person. In all my years of teaching I have never raised my voice in the classroom. I've been called names, had students ignore me, had them call each other names, had a near fistfight in my room, and had students disrupt my teaching with note passing, talking, texting, and more. But despite these provocations, I've never talked above my classroom voice. Not once. Nor have I ever yelled at my children or wife. I've never struck another human being in forty years since I punched Tracy Smith in the eye as an eight-year-old boy. (He must've had it coming.) But my snapping point came in the spring of 1998.

I was under a great deal of pressure that spring. In addition to having a wife, three kids, and a full-time teaching job, I was also a part-time youth pastor, high school golf coach, and general contractor for a $400,000 custom home. (For those keeping score, that was two full-time jobs and two part-time jobs.) For weeks on end I was up at dawn and at work until 10:00 p.m. I was exhausted. One afternoon my wife and I were having a discussion about some issue. I've long since forgotten it and I'm certain it was trivial. As we were discussing the issue, I became flooded with emotion. In my exhaustion I was too easily overwhelmed. We were talking in the upstairs bedroom and I knew I had to flee. So I went to the main floor to clear my head. But Tamara wanted closure. She deserved it from me, but I was unable to even articulate a clear thought. So she followed me down to the main floor to talk some more. I really wanted to help her feel better about what we were discussing, but I was incapable of giving her the closure she needed. I then went down to the basement. When I arrived at the bottom of the stairs, I looked up to see my wife still wanting to talk more. But I was done. Done with a capital D. Done as in D-O-N-E. Done as in "there is no way on earth I have another single word left in me to hear or speak." And in that moment I snapped and struck out. There is no way I would ever turn against my wife, so I took the full might of my strength out on the one thing closest to me—the handrail leading down to the basement. It was affixed to the wall ... and then it wasn't. I let out a guttural roar and, in a feat of near superhuman strength, pulled the handrail completely out of the wall and held it above my head as though I were in Asgard holding a lightning bolt. I was Thor! I was the god of the handrail! My wife let out a little squeal and ran upstairs. I eventually cooled off and in utter humiliation fixed the handrail. I've never looked like such a foolish jerk in all my life. What we both learned in that moment was I had a breaking point and neither of us was interested in seeing it again.

KNOWING WHEN TO ZIP IT

The reason I tell that story is to illustrate a very simple point—most males have a breaking point and every female needs to understand this. As adults we've had enough stress and arguments in our relationships that we may have seen this breaking point. But you know who doesn't understand that men sometimes need space or else they may snap and strike out? You guessed it—your daughter.

It is absolutely, crucially imperative that your daughter understands that *most* males have a breaking point, a point at which they might yell, scream, run, or worse—strike out physically. Even the most composed and self-disciplined male probably has a point at which he cannot take any more. Christine Ourada, of the abused women's shelter, put it more bluntly when she said, "Women need to know when to zip it. You need to be able to recognize the signs of what can become abusive." Ourada works with women coming out of abusive relationships. But I think this is good advice for any woman.

WHEN VIOLENCE IS A PATTERN

So far we have mostly discussed dating violence that may arise because of circumstances and unique situations. Unfortunately, there are some very broken boys in this world for whom abuse is not a spontaneous act of emotion but rather a sick, calculated pattern of behavior. It is these boys who present the most significant danger to girls.

There is a well-known anecdote about a frog in a pan of water on a stove top. If you turn up the heat slowly, the frog will cook to death without ever moving because the temperature change is imperceptible. It is death by degrees. Abuse is much the same way. Battered women don't become battered women overnight. It is often a slow process because the abuser's pattern of behavior is repetitive and escalating.

In many cases, the pattern of abuse begins with jealousy. To the uninitiated, jealousy masquerades as love. A girl might think it is sweet that a boy "cares" so much that he doesn't want her to talk with other guys. She might find it attractive that he "loves" her so much that he wants to have open access to her Facebook page. Or she may also be flattered by him because he wants to spend all of his time with her. Any of these behaviors can appear normal to a young girl. But they are not normal. They are the early signs of control.

According to Christine Ourada, "Control is the starting point for many abuses—where she can and can't go and the paranoia that accompanies that—'She is going to do something when I am not around.'" This control can take the form of trying to limit a girl's contact with her friends and family. It can also mean controlling her cell phone and text messages. In more extreme cases, a boy might exert control over when a girl leaves and how long she stays with him in a given place and time. Ourada put it this way: "A girl sees love, but what is really happening is she is being conquered."

Regardless of how the abuse starts, it can take many different forms and will escalate over time. Ourada stated, "I think abuse escalates from the first thought, *I want to hurt her* ... with each threshold getting easier to cross."

I believe an abuser begins with a small action. Perhaps it is hardly perceptible signs of jealousy and control. Then it metastasizes to verbal abuse. From there it can expand to emotional abuse and coercion. This paves the way for physical abuse: holding down, pushing, punching, and worse. As Ourada pointed out, each threshold, once crossed, makes it easier to cross the next. This was exactly what happened to Lisa.

LISA'S STORY

Lisa is a twenty-eight-year-old who spent over three years in a violently abusive relationship. We met because she was working with Christine Ourada and her staff in order to recover and rebuild her life. Lisa comes from a privileged background. She was adopted as an infant and had loving parents who took care of her. She went to church, graduated from high school, and by all accounts was a "normal" teenage girl. But Lisa had what I call a broken picker. She always chose boys who were damaged goods with a track record of significant problems: felons, gang members, drug addicts, and abusers. She told me, "I always found guys who were in trouble or needed help or came from hurt backgrounds. I thought I could fix them, but really I was trying to direct away my own problems. Then I didn't have to concentrate on me."[9]

Lisa says now that the core of her problem was that she believed she was worthless. I believe that in general people seek out partners who are about as emotionally healthy as they are. A girl who thinks she is worthless will often be attracted to a boy who feels he is worthless too. They may manifest their feelings of worthlessness in different ways—she may be weak and vulnerable, and he may be controlling and manipulative. Not a good combination. One psychologist described it this way: "When you lower your standards you are in fact worse than alone, you now have a liability: you have done picked up a dependent."[10] A fixer boy is not only a dependent; he can be a mortal enemy as well.

Jacquelyn:
To the untrained eye, the most put-together, self-sufficient, and confident girl can be in the most tumultuous relationship.

Take for example my friend from high school. She was an accomplished student, a talented athlete, and for all intents and purposes a very put-together young woman. She was kind, smart, loving, and a loyal friend. All in all, she was a really impressive person.

Despite all this, she had a string of just the *worst* boyfriends! Her most horrible choice was three years older than she was. He was a pathological liar and a cheater, and she stayed with him far past the time any other reasonable person would. She kept it secret for most of their relationship, but he was also terribly abusive. You would never have guessed it in a million years, because they acted as if they had the perfect high school romance. What I am trying to say is that anyone can fall victim to the broken picker, even your daughter. Despite your best efforts, there is a chance that your daughter could end up with a pretty bad guy. Keep this in mind as you read further.

"WE ACCEPT THE LOVE WE THINK WE DESERVE"

In the teen novel *The Perks of Being a Wallflower* one of the characters utters one of the most profound lines ever written about dating violence: "We accept the love we think we deserve."[11] This is the heart of the abuse story. When I talked with Lisa about her abuse, she said, "I thought I was bad. I thought the treatment was what I deserved."

Lisa's abuse began only a few weeks after she and her boyfriend got together. Because she had a child from a previous relationship, her new boyfriend began pressuring her to have a child so their relationship would be "equal" to her previous one. Jealous over her previous relationship, he coerced and even sexually assaulted her. And then when she got pregnant, he ramped up the control.

She said, "When I was out of town for the weekend, he moved into my apartment. He became very controlling and I wasn't allowed to have friends. I wasn't allowed to talk to my family. Every friend I had he would try to convince me why I shouldn't be friends with them and why he was mad at them. He would always find a reason to hate my parents. He wouldn't allow me to work because he didn't want me to have a paycheck. Even though he didn't have a license, he would take my car to work so I couldn't go anywhere."

This controlling behavior gave way to emotional abuse. Her boyfriend grew increasingly cruel. "If he came home from work and his laundry wasn't done, he would flip out on me. If I couldn't magically figure out what he wanted for dinner, he would start screaming at me. He would say things like 'If you really loved me ...' or 'You don't treat me like a man.'"

Then he started stalking her. He would secretly videotape her and obsess over the thought that she was cheating on him. "When I bought a car I had the salesperson's phone number on my cell phone. My boyfriend kept calling him over and over one night until midnight. Finally the salesperson answered and my boyfriend figured out I wasn't cheating." He would routinely wake up Lisa in the night and accuse her of being unfaithful.

In time his abuses became physical. When Lisa was six months pregnant, she tried to leave the house. He blocked the exit and threw her on the ground. "I was in complete shock the first time he hit me, and I locked myself in the bathroom. In the morning I left and went to my parents' house."

But in Lisa's emotionally weakened state she was not able to stay away from her abuser. "I knew the right thing was to stay away, but I would always let his craziness bring me right back."

Throughout her abuse, Lisa's ever-plummeting belief in her own value fueled her numerous returns to her abuser. "Every time he would come back in my life, he would say, 'You're worthless and not a good mom. You don't deserve your own daughter.' He would get in my head, and my own sense of value would go down more and more. I just completely gave up. After the physical abuse started, I lost the ability to stand up for myself. I don't know how it happened or when it happened. But when I look back now, it was so obvious. I don't know how I let him take so much control."

The control did not end for over three years. It wasn't until the man was jailed for his abuse that she was finally able to break free. When I asked her how she was going to rebuild her own value, she said, "My faith. Dealing with things from my childhood and accepting ownership of the things I can take ownership of. And for the rest, accepting that those things were not my fault and that they don't define me."

I then asked her what advice she would give to a girl who was being abused. She replied, "No matter what his reason, or what you think the reason is, there is no right for him to abuse you. You are more valuable than that."

All I can say is "Amen."

This is a sobering chapter, particularly if you have concerns that your daughter is at risk of being in an abusive relationship. But there are some things you can do to educate her about the early signs of abuse and to help her feel safe so that she will always come to you for support and advice when she needs it.

PREPARING YOUR DAUGHTER FOR FUTURE HAPPINESS
BE HER PROTECTOR

I know I've said this before, but it bears repeating. As hard as it is, don't react when your daughter comes to you with information you find alarming. She may shut down if she sees you are angry or upset (and I don't mean just at her!), and in the future she may not feel she can come to you.

Jacquelyn:
Once in high school, I was at a sleepover at a friend's house and things started to get weird. I was uncomfortable, but it was the middle of the night. I called my dad and he drove right over to get me. If your daughter ever finds herself in a tight spot, she needs to know that you are quick to rush to her defense, even if that means running down the hallway in your undies. I suggest having a chat with your daughter that goes something along the lines of "I will come to your rescue, without hesitation. No matter what."

No matter what kind of trouble I have gotten into, my parents have never freaked out. They have again and again taken in bad news from me with grace and love and have always made me feel safe. Because of this, I have complete confidence that I can tell them anything and get their help for how to get out of a sticky situation, no matter what it is.

Even though I didn't always realize it when I was in high school, my parents have always been my safe place.

TEACH HER THE EARLY SIGNS OF ABUSE

Hopefully your daughter will never need to access this list, but it's important that you have it and share it with her more than once.[12] A boyfriend may be a potential abuser if:

- You are afraid of him.
- He criticizes you and puts you down.
- You would be embarrassed if anyone saw how he treated you.
- He has a bad or unpredictable temper.
- He is excessively jealous or suspicious.
- He is very possessive.
- He controls your movements or activities.
- He keeps you from seeing friends or family.
- He limits your access to communication and social media.
- He blames you for his anger.

ENCOURAGE HER TO HAVE A ZERO-TOLERANCE POLICY TOWARD ABUSE

Around the time I was writing this chapter, I discovered a bird's nest in my front yard. A lesser goldfinch had taken up residence with its three hatchlings in the lower branches of a laceleaf maple. By pulling the branch down just slightly, you could see right into the nest. For a couple of weeks we enjoyed watching the featherless pink babies crane their necks up for the possibility of food. But soon they were covered in feathers. Not realizing that the hatchlings were now fledglings ready to leave the nest, I pulled the branch down for my daily peek into the bird world when, suddenly, three birds went flying in all different directions. They could not fly far, but they were fast. Before I could scoop them up, they were well hidden in the underbrush of my yard. In the mind of a bird I was the ultimate threat, and their response was to fly away and seek safety. This is precisely the response you should train your daughter to have at the first sign of abuse. All parents need to encourage their daughters to have a zero-tolerance policy for abuse.

In the United States more than three women are killed by their husbands or boyfriends every day.[13] Some of these women stayed with their significant other because they thought he would stop the abuse. But the truth about domestic abuse is undeniable: *if a woman is physically assaulted by her male partner, it will very likely happen again.*

Your daughter needs to understand this key truth about abuse. For an abuser, the best indicator of future behavior is past behavior. I tell teens all the time, "If you enjoy being screamed at, stick around; there will be more on the way. If you like being pushed and held down, then stay in that relationship because there will be more coming. If you enjoy being kicked and hit, then forgive the other person and don't leave, because it will be worse next time."

If a boy she is dating ever hit or kicked one of my daughters, I would want the first time to be the last time. So, I've told both of them, "If this ever happens to you, please come to me. I'll protect you and make sure it never happens again." Each of our daughters is precious and must be taught to fly away at the slightest bit of control, manipulation, or abuse. Men don't spontaneously decide to kill their partners. Thresholds have to be crossed. Men kill their partners as the final act in a very ugly play. Your daughter needs to stop the process before it ever gets started by flying away at the outset of abuse. She is far too valuable to let herself be harmed.

EDUCATE HER ABOUT HOW BOYS HANDLE STRESS AND WHEN SHE NEEDS TO ZIP IT

There are three things you need to teach your daughter about boys.

1. She needs to know if she can't get closure within the first ten to fifteen minutes of a discussion with a boy, she should move on. Maybe the issue could be brought up at a later time, or maybe the issue could be set aside permanently. She should know to move on if the boy looks like he has shut down and is beginning to flood emotionally. More words will not help the situation. They will, in fact, make it worse.

2. She should never stop a boy when he is walking away from her. There is a reason he is walking away. He can feel that he has reached his snapping point. The train is running full steam ahead with no brakes, and she is in danger of getting run over.

3. Under no circumstance should she ever hit a boy. This may be obvious, but one meta-study, a study of the studies, reports that girls are just as likely as boys to hit the other person in a relationship.[14] I think many of these "hits" are expressions of frustration rather than

full-strength blows. It is also true the average teenage girl doesn't possess the strength and size to seriously injure the average teenage boy, and therefore these hits are less serious. Herein lies the problem: she might hit him, but if he reacts, he has the capacity to do very serious harm to her. There is never, ever, ever an excuse for a boy to hit a girl, but if he is flooded with emotions and she strikes, he may strike back and hurt her.

Please do not read these three suggestions and take from them that I in any way condone violence against women. I need to say this again so my meaning is clear. It is never acceptable for a man to hit a woman. *Never*. But it is important for a girl to understand that some boys have poor impulse control and might be dangerous if the situation is sufficiently emotional and ugly. If we don't teach our daughters these few simple tips, they may find themselves in harm's way.

IF YOU SUSPECT PHYSICAL ABUSE, ACT FIRST, ASK QUESTIONS LATER

Though there is an inherent risk in standing against your daughter's boyfriend, you must be forceful if you suspect abuse. At the first sign of emotional or physical abuse, be prepared to get your teen out of that relationship at all costs. If that means moving across the country with her, do it. If that means confronting the boyfriend or his parents, do it. If that means bribing the boy to go away, do it. If your daughter is in harm's way, now is not the time for timidity and politeness. I'd rather be wrong and have to apologize than have to bury a child.

This is a tough chapter to read, so I think it fitting to end on a positive note. At the time of this writing, Lisa, the abuse survivor highlighted earlier in the chapter, has been free from abusive relationships for over two years. She is raising her children, maintaining a steady job, and growing stronger every day. In many ways she is a walking and talking miracle. It is my hope that one day no one's daughter will ever have to suffer abuse at the hands of any man. (If you would like to support the work Christine Ourada is doing with victimized women, you can visit her rescue's website at www.portlandrescuemission.org.)

QUESTIONS FOR REFLECTION

1. How have you let your daughter know that you are available when she is at her lowest point? In what ways are you open to your daughter sharing her vulnerabilities with you?
2. What do you think your daughter would do if she were abused in a relationship?

QUESTIONS FOR YOU AND YOUR DAUGHTER TO DISCUSS

1. How do boys and girls handle relationship stress differently? How can that pose a danger to you?
2. What would you do if a boy ever harmed you?
3. Why is it imperative that you break up with your boyfriend if he ever abuses you?

4. What are things your boyfriend could do or say that would immediately cause you to end the relationship?
5. What are some early-warning signs that a boy might be abusive?

LOOKING AHEAD TO THE NEXT CHAPTER

Fortunately, most girls won't experience the insanity of an on-again,
off-again relationship or the abuse that can accompany it. But after
their relationships end, many girls quickly jump into another relationship because they believe dating myth #9: *A rebound relationship
is just what I need.*

Dating Myth #9

A Rebound Relationship Is Just What I Need

Shelly, age seventeen, told me, "Sixth grade was the first year that my friend Blair got a boyfriend. She was the first of all our friends to get a boyfriend. Their relationship lasted about two months, with one breakup in the middle. They soon broke up officially, and we figured everything would go back to the way it was. But it didn't. Next came another boyfriend, and then another, and then another. Each of these relationships was one after another with only a few weeks between. She was addicted to being in a relationship. I once pointed it out to her and she said, 'I am a serial dater.' The worst part of all is that while she is in each serious relationship she has the next one lined up. Now I am scared because the next person she has lined up is one of my best friends—and he deserves better than being a Band-Aid, the next victim of her addiction."

In drug counseling there is an acronym known as HALT: hungry, angry, lonely, and tired. Counselors use it to help addicts recognize when they are most likely to relapse and also to remind them about what to do: halt. If love is like an addiction, then a teenage girl fresh off a breakup is in danger of relapse. She needs a "fix."

Just after the breakup a girl may be hungry, angry, lonely, and tired. Her hunger can be both physical and emotional. The anger she feels can be directed outward to her ex or inward to her own self for the role she played in the relationship coming to an end. Her loneliness is real and palpable. She is often emotionally worn out and physically exhausted from a lack of sleep. It is when she is HALT that she is most likely to make a bad choice. Other than getting back together with her ex, the worst choice she could make is to jump into another relationship without giving her heart time to heal.

Jacquelyn:

I remember going through a breakup and checking my phone almost obsessively for texts from my ex. There was something especially sad about a cell phone screen with no new notifications. I wanted to find another boyfriend because I knew that I didn't want to take my ex back, and I needed someone to pay attention to me, love me, and occupy my time and thoughts. One of my regrets about going underground about my boyfriends is that it prevented me from accessing the help my parents could have given me during this time.

SHE NEEDS A BAND-AID

There is no question that after a breakup a girl is wounded—and every wound needs a Band-Aid. If a girl refuses to get back together with her ex-boyfriend, her Band-Aid of choice then becomes a new relationship. This new relationship will raise her levels of dopamine and oxytocin, initially making her feel better because she gets to feel those early-stage euphoric feelings again.

Have you ever noticed how common it is for people to match up a friend who is recently divorced to someone else they know? The message our culture gives to someone who has just broken up is that he or she is supposed to "bounce back," "get back on the field," or "get back out there." You can bet that your daughter is hearing the message that the best way to get over her boyfriend is to find a new one. But it is not that simple.

Over time the new relationship will move out of the all-consuming lust stage (hedonic adaptation at work), and the experiences of her previous relationship along with her unresolved feelings and new questions may emerge. For example, if her previous boyfriend cheated on her, those memories and feelings will invariably manifest themselves in the new relationship. Or maybe she has not come to terms with her own failings in her previous relationship. We talked earlier about the past uglying up the present. I believe this happens in rebound relationships. In addition, hedonic adaptation takes hold, and the lustful feeling subsides in the new relationship; the "stickiness" of the Band-Aid wears off.

So even if a rebound relationship can appear to be a good thing in the beginning, over time the emotional lift it gives will dissipate. This is but one of the problems with rebound relationships.

THE PROBLEM WITH REBOUND RELATIONSHIPS
NO LESSON LEARNED

From my perspective, rebound relationships are mostly an exercise in pain avoidance. I'm not meaning to be critical here, because we all do differing things to avoid pain. Some are healthy, like confiding in friends, seeking counseling, and reading books on the subject. These approaches focus on creating resolution and acceptance. But others are not so healthy—things like overeating, blaming, and self-medicating with alcohol and drugs. These are strategies employed to distract or cover up the pain a person is feeling.

I like what legendary advice columnist Ann Landers said regarding drinking away pain: "People who drink to drown their sorrow should be told that sorrow knows how to swim."[1] A girl in a rebound relationship may be trying to drown her pain in a new relationship, but no matter how much she drinks from the glass of a new relationship, the pain will still be floating just below the surface. When the drink has been exhausted, she will be left holding a bitter, pain-filled glass.

It is never a good idea to forget an ex-boyfriend by getting a new boyfriend. Getting over a painful experience involves more than moving on; it involves learning. What is the good of a painful experience if it doesn't inform future decision making? If you never fully feel the pain, how can you learn from it? This doesn't mean we have to beat ourselves up over our bad decisions and wallow in our pain, but it does mean we have to give our pain time to teach us the lessons we are supposed to learn.

This maxim is very true after a breakup:

Emotional Pain + Rational Thought = Learning

This is how all people learn best. We think about the things that have hurt us, and we learn from the experiences. We make better choices. We avoid those situations in the future. We treat others better because we have learned from our past failures. When a girl jumps right into another relationship, she short-circuits this important process. As a result, she is prone to make the same mistakes again. Like Shelly in the beginning of the chapter, she may become a serial rebounder, moving from relationship to relationship.

Because a rebound relationship does not allow for healing and learning from the previous relationship, a serial rebounder can be left with many unhealed wounds. An open wound is dangerous and leaves a person at risk for serious complications.

IT DEVALUES THE OTHER PERSON

When a girl is in recovery mode after a breakup, her emotional state is unsteady. For understandable reasons she has many emotional needs to be met. Loneliness, fear, anxiety, and depression are common post-breakup problems that need to be resolved. She isn't in much of a position to give to another human being. When she enters into a rebound relationship, she is using the other person to help heal her wounds. She may not even recognize or know she is doing this, but she is using him nonetheless.

Jacquelyn:

I had some really awesome guy friends throughout high school, and I watched many of them get used in this way. One of them was my friend Brian. He'd had a crush on Tina since around the fifth grade, but she was never interested in him until she went through a serious breakup. Brian didn't understand that Tina was using him to alleviate the emotional pain she was in, and he was hurt that she was never really emotionally available to him. This rebound relationship didn't last very long, but the pain it caused Brian lingered for years. I think it is important to explain to your daughter that not only is a rebound bad for her, but also it is unkind to the boy she is in essence using.

Without speaking words, Tina was saying to Brian, "I need you to fill my needs, and your needs are secondary." He was a means to her end. This is a problem. An approach like this does not honor the human value of the other person. Healthy people do not enter into a relationship based only on what they can get; they enter into it based on what they can give as well. People who understand they are valuable give to others because they are valuable too.

SENSE OF SELF GETS LOST

As a girl moves from relationship to relationship, she becomes a "we" time and again. This is perhaps one of the most dangerous aspects of a rebound relationship. Let me explain.

When I met Tamara, I was definitely a "me." I was a brash and cocky twenty-year-old college basketball player with dreams of a professional playing career. *My* vision for *my* future involved *me* chasing *my* dream. There was no thought given to a "we." But oh, how that all changed after Tamara and I dated for a few months and we grew more serious. I began to give up some of "me" and give it over to a "we." No longer did I define myself solely as an individual "me" but rather as part of "we." It is not that I had changed as a person. I was still me, but how I viewed myself had changed. My identity was now intertwined with my future wife's identity. This process only intensified after we were engaged and later married, to the point where I can now say I have happily been part of "we" for over twenty-eight years.

When a girl enters into a relationship, she becomes part of a "we." In a short-term dating relationship, which rarely goes beyond the first stage of relationships (lust), a girl doesn't give up too much of herself to the "we." But in a longer-term relationship, one that makes it past the second stage (attraction) and into the third (attachment), she gives over larger parts of herself to the "we." (It is important to note that this process of becoming a "we" happens entirely too fast in too-much, too-soon relationships.) This can be dangerous for a still maturing girl. At a time in her life when she should be clarifying her values and cementing her sense of self, she is enmeshing herself into another person's life. As a girl moves from relationship to relationship, she becomes a "we" time and again. When that relationship ends, the "we" gets broken and immediately combined with a new "we." Each move to a new relationship can cause a girl to lose sight of her "me."

As she moves from relationship to relationship, a girl will often lose sight of her core values as she takes on the core values of each new boyfriend. Her core values get buried anew in each relationship, and they may remain buried unless she breaks away from the cycle of rebound relationships. A girl who constantly molds herself to the expectations of her current boyfriend and gives over her individuality to the "we" is scarcely recognizable to those around her. It is as though the girl everyone once knew has disappeared.

Jacquelyn:

I am a bit of a people pleaser, and this was especially true of me in high school. I spent so much time conforming to the values of my boyfriends that I had lost sight of what I loved and what I was about. I did things that I probably wouldn't have done otherwise, listened to different music, even did my hair differently. Because I jumped from relationship to relationship, my inner compass was no longer pointing due north. It's hard enough for high school girls to understand their own developing personality and identity. It became all the more complicated for me when I was in a relationship, and it felt impossible when I bounced from one boyfriend to another one. In my early twenties, when I woke up to what I had been doing, I spent a lot of time getting back in touch with myself.

When a girl loses sight of her "me," she can lose sight of her own value. Instead of anchoring her goodness in the fact that she is valuable and strong simply because she is made in the image of God, she may define herself and her goodness by being in a relationship. As we said earlier, she is "bad" and worthless when she is single, but she is "good" and valuable when in a relationship. This manifest weakness leaves her vulnerable to many dangers.

If what my rabbi friend says about *echad* and what John Mark Comer describes as the "primal connection" is true, a sexually active girl going from relationship to relationship is more than just one "we." As she becomes one with a boy, she leaves something of herself behind and takes on something moving forward. In each successive relationship, her "we" is not just two people; it includes all of the boys she has been one with.

This may have much to do with the fact that there is a relationship between the number of sex partners a girl has in her lifetime and the likelihood that she will have a lifelong, stable marriage. A serial rebounder has an increased chance of experiencing more relationship failure in the future, including in marriage.

It has been said that the definition of insanity is doing the same thing over and over and expecting different results. A girl on the rebound is very much doing the same thing over and over and expecting different results. She hopes that each new relationship will bring happiness and stability. But the results are usually the same for her. Sadly, the end result of each rebound relationship is usually more heartache and another rebound relationship around the bend.

PREPARING YOUR DAUGHTER FOR FUTURE HAPPINESS
ENCOURAGE HER TO IDENTIFY DEAL BREAKERS

One of my favorite TV characters is Sue Heck from *The Middle*. Sue is an indefatigable, supergeek sixteen-year-old. In one episode she has a conversation that goes like this:

Sue: Mom, guess what. Brad said a boy likes me …

Mom: ... Wow. And you like him too?

Sue: Duh. He likes me.

Mom: Yeah, I know he likes you, but do you like him back?

Sue: You heard he likes me, right?

Mom: Yeah, I got that, but do you like him?

Sue: I'm not following.

Mom: You know, Sue, just because a boy likes you doesn't mean you have to like him back.[2]

For Sue Heck, the quality of the boy makes no difference. If he likes her, then she likes him.

A girl on the rebound is much the same way. She often has a broken picker. Because she "needs" to get into another relationship, she doesn't apply any standards to the type of boy she chooses. She chooses the first guy who shows any interest in her. This is why we suggested earlier that your daughter create a list of qualities she is looking for in a boy. It's equally important she create a list of deal breakers.

Consider taking your daughter out for coffee or dessert and helping her develop this list. Such deal breakers would likely include drug and alcohol use, criminal behavior, bad grades, drastically different religious backgrounds, past history of poor relationships, and so forth. Her line of thinking should be something like this: *It doesn't matter how crazy hot he is, if he* _____, *I will not date him."* Or: *Even if he seems like the most wonderful guy in the world, if he believes* _____, *I will not spend time with him.*

It is vital that every girl have a list of deal breakers because it can help keep her out of a relationship that is not good for her. Revisit the list with her from time to time, and don't be afraid to offer a suggestion or two.

Jacquelyn:

Man, I wish I would have had a list of deal breakers when I was in high school! (Yes, I definitely have one now!) Making a list and measuring every potential suitor by it may have saved me from quite a bit of heartbreak. Since my dating life was a secret, I didn't have the benefit of my parents' guidance in this area, yet I sure could have used it. When I was in high school, I think my list of deal breakers would have been something like this:

- If he is not a Christian, don't go out with him!
- If he drinks or does drugs, don't go out with him!
- If he is failing his classes, don't go out with him!
- If he has had more than one girlfriend, don't go out with him!
- If he is not generally kind to everyone, don't go out with him!

TEACH HER THE 50 PERCENT RULE

A girl fresh out of a relationship needs to consider how much time she has had to heal before she enters a new relationship. The 50 percent rule may be a good standard. I made up this rule, and it says you will be single for 50 percent of the time you were dating before you start dating again.

For example, if your daughter was in an exclusive relationship for ninety days, she won't date another boy for at least forty-five days. If she was in a serious dating relationship for a year, then she needs to be single for six months. This period of time will allow her to bring to the surface the "me" who was submerged inside the "we" during that previous relationship. This may be a difficult guideline to convince your daughter to abide by, but it is certainly one worth talking about with her. Hopefully, she will see this as a way to ensure that she won't lose sight of herself, her goals, and her needs. As my own experience with Jacquelyn shows, we cannot force our children to follow our rules. But I encourage you to work to support your daughter after a break so that she is not tempted to jump into another relationship.

I'm sure there is a point at which the 50 percent rule becomes too much. I've been with my wife twenty-eight years, and if she were to pass away I don't think I would need to wait fourteen years to date again; but then again, neither would I show up at her funeral with a date. A teen fresh off a breakup needs time to reestablish her life outside of the dating world before she enters it again.

Of all the poor advice I hear young girls give one another, perhaps the poorest is "You should put yourself out there and start seeing someone again." The complete short-circuiting of the learning and healing process can have dire consequences for a young woman. It is my hope that you now have the information and tools to guide your daughter through a breakup and help her avoid a rebound relationship.

QUESTIONS FOR REFLECTION

1. Have you ever been in a rebound relationship? What did you learn about yourself from that experience that you can share with your daughter?

2. Has your daughter ever been in a rebound relationship? What do you think caused her to do this?

3. Is your daughter a serial rebounder? If so, what steps might you take to help her break the cycle?

4. How are you going to be proactive in teaching your daughter about the importance of being patient after a relationship has ended?

QUESTIONS FOR YOU AND YOUR DAUGHTER TO DISCUSS

1. What is a girl looking for when she starts a rebound relationship?
2. What are the benefits of taking time off before starting another relationship? What are the dangers of not waiting long enough?
3. What is the proper amount of time between relationships?
4. What are some of your deal breakers in a boyfriend?
5. How do girls lose themselves when they are in a relationship? How can a girl maintain her individuality while in a relationship?

LOOKING AHEAD TO THE NEXT CHAPTER

When a girl is always on the rebound, moving from relationship to relationship, she soon will become a serial dater. She may justify her behavior by telling herself that all of her relationships will help her make better choices in the future. Or that having several serious relationships will help her have a successful marriage. Sadly, nothing could be further from the truth, as the serial dater is guided by dating myth #10: *Serial dating and living together will help me stay married.*

Serial Dating and Living Together Will Help Me Stay Married

The life cycle of the Pacific salmon is hard to believe. They are born in inland streams throughout the Pacific Northwest and Canada. When they reach maturity, they venture out to the ocean for several years and then begin their arduous journey inland to spawn. The average journey back is 150 miles, with some species swimming upstream for more than two thousand miles. As the salmon head home to spawn, they swim against the current every inch of the way. Some salmon climb as many as seven thousand feet in the journey. As they return to their spawning grounds, they encounter dangers from otters, bears, eagles, and other predators. In addition to predators, salmon must climb up fish ladders and waterfalls. They have been known to leap as high as twelve feet up a waterfall. When the salmon reach their final destination, they spawn and die, giving rise to a new generation to carry on the cycle.[1] The fact that any salmon can travel against the current and overcome the obstacles with success is incredible.

Sometimes I feel like a salmon swimming upstream. The cultural stream flows one way and I am swimming another. The American path to marriage is typified by many serious relationships, multiple sex partners, and at least one cohabitation prior to marriage. So far in this book I've presented arguments and research that suggest that the way our daughters often approach dating is toxic. I believe this toxicity is reflected in high divorce rates. Cohabitation rates are the highest in American history,[2] and conventional wisdom suggests that living together before marriage is a good idea in order to determine whether a couple can get along with each other.[3]

For most young Americans today the journey to marriage goes something like this: Their first foray into the world of relationships begins in middle school or junior high. By the time they graduate from high school, they have had at least one romantic relationship.[4] Most people lose their virginity in high school and have a number of hookups and more sex partners while in college. Once out of college, they have several significant relationships. During one or more of these, they live with their partner for a period of time before they eventually marry. (Nearly 75 percent of American women under the age of thirty have cohabited.[5])

This is the pathway our culture has laid out before our daughters. It has society's approval, and for most it is the expected path. But do serial relationships and living together really prepare you to have a good marriage? Though divorce rates are notoriously difficult to analyze,[6] it is safe to assume at least 40 percent of all marriages end in divorce, and the dissolution rates for cohabiters are substantially higher.[7] Clearly, all of this "practice" is not working very well.

While the majority of Americans have put their faith in living together as a necessary step to marriage, the research does not support this belief. In this chapter we will challenge the assumption that serial dating and living together will lead to more stable marital outcomes. I believe it is critical for our daughters to understand that what they likely hear every day about serial dating and living together is flat-out wrong.

SERIAL DATING ENCOURAGES PATTERNS THAT WORK AGAINST STABLE MARRIAGES

A serial dater is a person who is "all-in" from relationship to relationship. Like a gambler who has moved all his chips into the pot with the hope of victory, a girl who is all-in has moved her chips into the center of the table with this new relationship. In hope of finding a stable relationship, she is all-in with her time, finances, emotions, and body. With the average age of marriage for women now at twenty-seven years,[8] it's possible for a woman to have a half-dozen or more significant relationships prior to marriage, particularly if she began dating early and was engaged in TMTS (too-much, too-soon) relationships. If she is the norm in America, a young woman will have had several sex partners[9] and at least one live-in relationship prior to marriage.[10]

For argument's sake let's suppose a girl had six all-in relationships between the ages of sixteen and twenty-seven. As her final relationship enters the marriage stage, she will now be able to draw on the lessons she has learned from her previous five relationships. Just what has she learned?

I believe the most significant lesson she has learned is how to break up. If her all-in relationships were like mini-marriages, then she has learned from each of these unions that when things are difficult you break up. She may not have initiated any of the breakups, but she has learned the lesson well. Any married couple who has been together any length of time can tell you this is a bad lesson to learn. Most marriages have ebbs and flows in happiness. There may be extended times when marriage is just plain, old-fashioned hard work and not just flowers and sunshine. For a couple struggling through a season of discord, this lesson is not helpful. If a girl has learned this lesson well, she may be hurting herself by initiating a divorce. One study has found that unhappily married people who get divorced are no happier than those who remain in unhappy marriages. This study goes on to conclude that two-thirds of the couples who say they are unhappily married will rate themselves as happily married five years later.[11] It just may be that perseverance is the most important lesson one can learn when it comes to marital happiness.

Perhaps you are thinking, *Okay. I can buy that serial dating isn't good practice for marriage. But what about living together? Seems like couples who live together need to work out problems just like married folks do, and they enter marriage better equipped to handle the ebbs and flows.*

This is certainly the line of thinking I hear from my students. But does living together really prepare a person for marriage?

CAN ONE REALLY PRACTICE FOR MARRIAGE?

On the surface there seems a measure of truth in this belief. If you live with a person before marrying them, you could really discover what they are about and if they are a good fit for you. By living together, you might also pick up some communication skills that will help you in marriage. I think preparation for marriage is a noble goal, but I'm not sure it happens through living together.

As a single man I had only one serious relationship, and that was with my future wife. We spent a great deal of time together and formed a solid partnership before we got married. But I'm not sure anything could have ever fully prepared me for marriage. I suspect many people feel the same way. Marriage is such a dramatic change in your life that it requires quite a bit of adjustment. For me it felt like being in a Viper-class fighter launched from the *Battlestar Galactica*. (Sorry about another sci-fi reference. I can't help myself!) The changes in my life came mighty fast.

Young adults know their lives will change significantly when they get married, and understandably, most would like some measure of control and some confidence that they are doing the right thing. I think the modern American path to marriage as outlined earlier is, in part, an attempt to gain control of what is ultimately uncontrollable. This hope for assurance and control, however, is probably destructive to marriages in the long run.

For the sake of argument let us suppose one can actually become fully prepared for marriage. What, then, would be the best practice for marriage? In my mind the very best practice would be to have been married before. If one had been married before, then he or she would have learned all the important lessons and skills necessary to make another marriage work. What could be a better preparation for marriage than to learn from the mistakes of a previous marriage?

Well, as it turns out, almost anything. One source reports that divorce rates for first marriages are 41 percent, for second marriages 60 percent, and for third marriages 73 percent.[12] Presumably the pool of available data for those married four times is too small to offer much insight. So, if a previous marriage is not good practice for marriage, how about the next-best thing?

For millions of Americans the next-best thing is cohabitation. Conventional wisdom holds that if a couple eases in to marriage by living together, the chances of marital happiness are increased. According to one poll, only 27 percent of Americans are opposed to cohabitation.[13] And more than half of all couples will cohabit prior to marriage.[14] With each passing year cohabitation becomes the normative experience prior to marriage, particularly among the poor.[15] But does this lead to more stable marital outcomes?

If the vast body of research on the question is to be believed, then the answer is a resounding no. There are hundreds of studies on the topic, and there is scant evidence that cohabitation fosters more stable or happy marriages; in fact, the vast majority suggests just the opposite. One study analyzed decades of research around cohabitation and marital stability. This meta-study of nearly one thousand published articles from peer-reviewed journals reported that cohabitation was associated with "negative marital outcomes."[16] This meta-study did not seek, however, to draw a causal connection between the two. Another study took this finding a step further and focused on the marital outcomes for women as a result of cohabitation. Utilizing survey data from over sixty-five hundred women, this study had several significant conclusions that should inform your daughter's thinking about cohabitation.[17]

1. Having more than one sex partner prior to marriage *causes* higher divorce rates in the future. This causal connection is not based on the personality or thinking of the

person. It is based on the fact that a person has more than one sex partner prior to marriage.

2. Women who have more than one cohabiting relationship have higher divorce rates. This research concluded there was a *causal* connection between cohabitation, pre-marital sex, and marital instability. When talking about cohabitation and divorce, people often dismiss the connection by saying, "People who live together just aren't the marrying types." Or as it is commonly thought, "People who get married without living together are usually religious and less prone to divorce." (This is not true, as evangelical Christians have divorce rates nearly identical to the general population.[18]) Rather, *the act of cohabitation itself* causes divorce rates to rise. If your daughter wants to live with a man before she is married in order to increase her chances at staying married, she is very likely doing exactly the opposite of what she should be doing.

This last finding is echoed by another research project. The study used data from the Centers for Disease Control and Prevention, and while it did not seek to provide causal connections between numbers of sex partners and marital stability, it did provide associations between these two. According to the study, delaying first sex is positively associated with marital stability, reduced rates of STIs, and greater happiness. The most compelling finding in this study indicates that there is a *linear* relationship between the number of sexual partners and marital stability.[19] To put it more simply, the more boys a girl sleeps with prior to marriage, the greater her risk for marital instability. While the nature of this risk is unknown, one thing is clear: there is a connection that is hard to ignore.

So if cohabitation doesn't result in more stable marriages, why are unmarried couples living together? I think the answer is that few people question the status quo on cohabitation and most have bought into this myth without ever analyzing whether it is true.

The truth, as it turns out, is that there is a very strong case for marriage over cohabitation.

CHOOSING MARRIAGE OVER COHABITATION

For years marriage has been a cultural battleground between the left and the right, with Christian conservatives extolling the virtues of marriage. In this case, the religious folks have it right. By almost any quantifiable measure, marriage is a better form of partnership than cohabitation. For example:

- People in marriages live longer with better emotional well-being than those who cohabitate.[20]
- Marriages last much longer. Only about 13 percent of cohabiting couples make it past five years, while 77 percent of marriages do.[21]
- Children living with cohabiting biological parents are four times more likely to be abused than children living with married biological parents.[22]
- Women in cohabiting relationships are far more likely to suffer abuse than those in marriages.[23]

It may be impossible to determine why marriage has so many benefits. It may be that "marrying types" are less prone to some of the ills associated with those who cohabit. Or it may be that marriage fosters a better quality of life. It may require decades of research before we know the answers for sure. But if one were going to wager on the future happiness of his or her daughter, marriage seems the safer bet.

Jacquelyn:

I am the statistical outlier in my generation. When I tell people that I will never live with someone before I am married, they usually look at me like I have sprouted a second nose. People want to know how I could ever get to know a person if we don't live together first. I think it has a lot to do with what my parents taught me. They have always been very up front with the data, probably because they are both teachers! We were raised with the unshakable knowledge, backed by fact, that cohabitation was a bad idea. Like my mom always said, why buy the cow when you get the milk for free? If I want to get married, there are some things I just shouldn't do without a ring on that finger. It's just the truth!

In our culture, living together is seen as a natural step between dating and marriage. But as I was growing up, my parents taught my siblings and me that instead of being good practice, living together was essentially a death sentence for marriage. When I was in high school, they told me this at least once a month, and I am grateful because the message stuck with me!

PREPARING YOUR DAUGHTER FOR FUTURE HAPPINESS

Much of what this book has been about is advice and information designed to steer a girl away from serial dating and to help her establish healthy dating patterns. Understanding human value, following the 50 percent rule, building a rich and varied life, and avoiding TMTS relationships are all ways of not getting caught up in serial dating. But as important as all of these may be, helping your daughter develop a mind-set of singleness might be the most important.

HELP HER CULTIVATE A MIND-SET OF SINGLENESS

Men today are very slow to come to the marriage table. They are marrying later and later. Just ask a single thirty-year-old woman, and she will likely tell you that many of the men she knows are in a state of perpetual boyhood with not much interest in marriage. With more and more people putting off marriage until later in life, it's important that you help your daughter cultivate a mind-set of singleness.

Teach her from an early age that being single is not a curse. Single girls often hear the message that their status is bad. It can come from peers, media, family, church, and others. A girl who feels pressured to be in a relationship may lower her standards and conform to a norm that she is not comfortable with. As a parent, you need to teach your daughter the message that it is okay to be single, which can go a long way in helping her swim upstream against the cultural current, particularly as she grows older. If she is going to avoid serial dating and cohabitating before marriage, she will have to go through extended times of singleness. If you perpetuate the idea that she has to be in a relationship, she may end up in a series of all-in relationships that do not serve her well in her later married life.

MAKE IT CLEAR YOU'LL OFFER NO SUPPORT IF SHE COHABITATES

Jacquelyn:

My parents have always made it abundantly clear that cohabitation is a nonstarter. They went so far as to say that they would be extremely angry and disappointed if any of us kids made this choice. What my parents have always told me is that if you aren't ready to get married, then you definitely aren't ready to live together. In high school, I didn't ever have a job other than the occasional babysitting gig. In my parents' minds, my job was to be a good, well-rounded student, not to go out and get a job. I know that financially this was a sacrifice for them, but looking back on my high school years I am especially grateful for their determination to support me.

Now that I'm in my twenties, I can tell you that for many people my age the pressure to live together comes from the daunting task of maintaining two separate households: rent, bills, and so on. If your daughter is ever in this situation, I encourage you to think of some creative solutions for alleviating the financial stress on her. Are you able to help her financially with some of her expenses so she can continue to live on her own? Can you create a space in your home where she feels independent yet supported? This decision might be a bit down the road for your teenage daughter, but it should be something that you plan for now. My parents were my parents in high school, and they still are my parents now as an adult.

USE THIS BOOK TO SPARK IDEAS THAT LEAD TO WISE CHOICES

I believe that when a girl follows the basic principles about dating that are outlined in this book, she will make wise choices. Yes, she will make mistakes along the way, but the bend of her decision making will be toward wisdom. These truths can form a powerful yes in her life. And for each yes, there is a corresponding no.

"Yes, I know that I am valuable" is coupled with "No, you will never hurt me again."

"Yes, I know that my feelings are fallible" goes along with "No, I won't let my emotions carry me away."

"Yes, I understand real love takes time" is followed by "No, I can't be in love yet."

"Yes, I know love and sex are different" is met with "No, I won't sleep with you."

Making wise choices is hard, no question about it. If making wise choices were easy, many of the world's problems would disappear overnight. Most of the time saying no involves resisting some temptation. It is like the old cartoon image of a devil on one shoulder and an angel on the other. Each no is an internal debate to make the right choice. If your daughter is to make wise choices, a burning yes must be inside of her. Most people don't have a burning yes. At best they have a smoldering maybe. Your daughter needs your help if she is to have a burning yes inside of her. You are the spark to light a burning yes in her. The fire of yes can happen only when you introduce the spark of new ideas to your daughter. I hope this book can be a resource to spark the fire of yes in your daughter.

QUESTIONS FOR REFLECTION

1. What have you taught your daughter about cohabitation? Does it reflect the research about cohabitation?
2. What steps can you take today (even if your daughter isn't yet dating) to help ensure that your daughter will avoid cohabitation?

QUESTIONS FOR YOU AND YOUR DAUGHTER TO DISCUSS

1. Why might living with your boyfriend before marriage be a bad idea?
2. How do you think a couple could prepare for marriage besides living together?
3. What is the message a man is sending to you when he is willing to live with you but not marry you? Is this message consistent with the idea that you are valuable?

Conclusion

Margaret and Rollie

I have a friend named Rollie. I met him at the health club where I work out; or maybe I should say he met me. The first time I talked to him, I was swimming laps as he was walking laps in the pool. I stopped swimming for a moment, and Rollie said, "Say, friend, your hard work is really inspiring to me." I liked how that sounded: "Say, friend." No one talks like that much anymore, so I decided to put my goggles on top of my head and have a short conversation. I'm really glad I did because Rollie has become a good friend. What I learned that first day was that Rollie was eighty-eight years old. That impressed me. He doesn't look a day over sixty-five and works out six days a week. (And he was the one saying *I* inspired *him*. Are you kidding me?)

Rollie and I had breakfast one morning, and I learned a great deal about him. He grew up during the Great Depression and served as a crew member in a bomber escort in World War II, flying many missions over Japan. He eventually lived in Japan for over thirty years, where he served as a missionary. He is kind, insightful, and extremely encouraging to those people he encounters. With his gentle spirit and twenty-four-hour-a-day smile, he is the kind of person who always makes you feel better for having spent time with him. I had him come and speak to my history classes about his life, and the students were blown away. At eighty-eight he was jumping over electrical cords as he talked about his experiences in World War II. Rollie has a spark in him that defies explanation. He exudes love. After talking with the students, he insisted on shaking each student's hand or hugging them and thanking them for coming. There is a lot to love about Rollie; he is truly a great man.

They say behind every great man there is a great woman. In this case her name is Margaret. I met Margaret for the first time over lunch with her and Rollie. Margaret is eighty-two years old and a breast cancer survivor. In addition to raising two boys, she spent her working life as a recording artist, music arranger, and piano instructor. The first time I met her, I couldn't help but notice how well put together she was. She had a beautiful twinkle in her eye, clear and lovely skin, and not a hair was out of place. As we talked, I was impressed by both her humility and her genuine affection for her husband. Margaret and Rollie sat side by side in the Shari's restaurant booth, periodically glancing at each other during our conversation, and you could just see the love they have for each other. They were not long, loving gazes, but rather quick looks at each other that said, "I'm so lucky to have you." I am not exaggerating when I say you could feel the love between them. To experience it was beautiful and deeply moving.

Margaret and Rollie have been married for over sixty years, and I wanted to know how they were able to do it. Specifically, what did they do when they were young that helped make their marriage last so long? We talked for nearly two hours that afternoon. What I came away with from our time together is Margaret and Rollie dated with a plan and made good choices before they were married. These were two people who were happy when they were young and dating, and they are happy today in the twilight of their lives. They were able to answer the question of how you can date in the here and now and still be happy in the future. This is what *The 10 Myths of Teen Dating* is all about. How can we teach our daughters to date smart today so they can be happy tomorrow? Margaret and Rollie figured it out. This is what I want for my own daughters, and I hope it is what you want for yours. Hopefully you are well on your way to making that a reality for your own daughter.

Acknowledgments

This book would never have come to fruition without the unconditional love and support of my wife, Tamara. Not only has she been the best partner to go through life with, but she sacrificed immensely to the creation of the ten myths. My love for you remains deep and unabiding. Thank you for being the most wonderful mother to our children and teaching me more about relationships than any book or study ever could.

Dan and Jacquelyn would like to dedicate this book to the thousands of students who've helped shaped the teachings on the ten myths. Without your experiences, stories, reactions, and thoughts, none of this would have come to pass. A tremendous amount of gratitude also goes to our students, Jacquelyn's friends, and our acquaintances who lent us their tales. We hope that by sharing your experiences, girls can avoid repeating the same mistakes. Thank you for your honesty and willingness to be a part of the story.

We owe a debt of gratitude to the men and women who have given their time to read the book at various stages of the process. Dan's sisters, Christy and Kathy; his sister-in-law, Anne; and our good friend Ann Donaca-Sullivan all shared invaluable feedback. A special thank-you to Mary Rodeback for volunteering for the laborious task of initial editing. We appreciate it more than you know! We are thankful for Hugh Halter who answered many questions from Dan throughout the whole process. We were fortunate to be able to visit our friends Kim and Krickitt Carpenter, who have been huge supporters of this book. Thank you for your advice and guidance from the earliest days of this project.

A special thank-you to our literary agent, Tawny Johnson; Don Jacobson; and everyone at D.C. Jacobson for believing in a project by unknown authors. Without your belief in the message, none of this would have been possible. Although no longer with David C Cook, we owe a debt of gratitude to Ingrid Beck for advocating for our book to be published. Thank you for hearing our message and assuaging our fears and anxieties throughout the publication process.

As for David C Cook, we have greatly appreciated the opportunity to work with such a caring, motivated group of professionals. Thank you to Alice Crider for taking this project over the finish line and to Liz and Jack, our outstanding editors. You created order from what was at times chaotic, and we are forever in your debt.

Notes

INTRODUCTION: A DIFFERENT KIND OF DATING BOOK

1. "Sexual Exploitation and Substance Abuse," AlcoholRehab.com, accessed March 15, 2016, http://alcoholrehab.com/drug-addiction/sexual-exploitation-and -substance-abuse/.

DATING MYTH #1: IF I HAD A BOYFRIEND I WOULD BE HAPPY

1. Robert Holden, "The One Thing Every Parent Wants," Oprah.com, December 11, 2009, www.oprah.com/spirit/5-Keys-to-Your-Childs-Happiness.

2. "Ed Diener," Pursuit of Happiness, accessed March 15, 2016, www.pursuit-of -happiness.org/history-of-happiness/ed-diener/.

3. "Annual Happiness Index Again Finds One-Third of Americans Very Happy," Harris Poll, June 22, 2011, www.theharrispoll.com/health-and-life/Annual _Happiness_Index_Again_Finds_One-Third_of_Americans_Very_Happy.html.

4. "What Is Happiness?," WGBH Educational Foundation, accessed December 3, 2015, www.pbs.org/thisemotionallife/topic/happiness/what-happiness.

5. Daniel Kahneman and Angus Deaton, "High Income Improves Evaluation of Life but Not Emotional Well-Being," *Proceedings of the National Academy of Sciences of the United States of America* 107, no. 38 (2010), www.pnas.org/content/107/38/16489.abstract.

6. Gregg Easterbrook, *The Progress Paradox: How Life Gets Better While People Feel Worse* (New York: Random, 2003), xvi.

7. Graeme Wood, "Secret Fears of the Super-Rich," *Atlantic Monthly*, April 2011, www.theatlantic.com/magazine/archive/2011/04/secret-fears-of-the-super -rich/308419/.

8. Wood, "Secret Fears."

9. Matthew 19:16–22 and Luke 15:11–32, respectively.

10. "The U-Bend of Life," *Economist*, December 16, 2010, www.economist.com /node/17722567.

11. Christopher P. Niemiec, Richard M. Ryan, and Edward L. Deci, "The Path Taken: Consequences of Attaining Intrinsic and Extrinsic Aspirations in Post-College Life," US National Library of Medicine, June 2009, www.ncbi.nlm.nih.gov/pmc/articles/PMC2736104/.

12. Sonja Lyubomirsky, *The How of Happiness: A New Approach to Getting the Life You Want* (London: Penguin, 2007), 39.

13. Sonja Lyubomirsky, "Hedonic Adaptation to Positive and Negative Experiences," *Psychology Today*, April 8, 2010, www.psychologytoday.com/files /attachments/496/hedonic-adaptation-positive-experiences.pdf.

14. Vocabulary.com, s.v. "hedonism," accessed March 15, 2016, www.vocabulary.com/dictionary/hedonism.

15. Helen Fisher, *Why We Love: The Nature and Chemistry of Romantic Love* (New York: Henry Holt, 2004), 85–86.

16. "Martin Seligman," Pursuit of Happiness, accessed March 15, 2016, www.pursuit -of-happiness.org/history-of-happiness/martin-seligman-positive-psychology.

17. Salynn Boyles, "Happiness Is Contagious: Social Networks Affect Mood, Study Shows," WebMD, December 4, 2008, www.webmd.com/balance/news /20081204/happiness-is-contagious.

DATING MYTH #2: I SHOULD TRUST MY FEELINGS

1. "The Galileo Seven," *Star Trek*, NBC (January 5, 1967).

2. "What Are Little Girls Made Of?," *Star Trek*, NBC (October 10, 1966).

3. Louann Brizendine, *The Female Brain* (New York: Three Rivers, 2006), 37.

4. Brizendine, *Female Brain*, 51.

5. Brizendine, *Female Brain*, 51.

6. Catalina L. Toma, Jeffrey Hancock, and Nicole Ellison, "Separating Fact from Fiction: An Examination of Deceptive Self-Presentation in Online Dating Profiles," *Personality and Social Psychology Bulletin* 34, no. 8 (2008).

7. William Tooke and Lori Camire, "Patterns of Deception in Intersexual and Intrasexual Mating Strategies," Academia, accessed March 15, 2016, www.academia.edu/808354/Patterns_of_deception_in_intersexual_and _intrasexual_mating_strategies.

8. Brizendine, *Female Brain*, 64.

9. Wade C. Rowatt, Michael R. Cunningham, and Perri B. Druen, "Deception to Get a Date," *Personality and Social Psychology Bulletin* 24, no. 11 (November 1998), http://psp.sagepub.com/content/24/11/1228.abstract?patientinform-links=yes&legid=sppsp;24/11/1228, doi: 10.1177/01461672982411009.

10. Sarah Allen and Kerry Daly, "The Effects of Father Involvement: An Updated Research Summary of the Evidence," Father Involvement Research Alliance, May 2007, www.fira.ca/cms/documents/29/Effects_of_Father_Involvement.pdf.

11. Daniel Goleman, *Emotional Intelligence*, 10th anniv. ed. (New York: Bantam Books, 2006), 83, 96.

12. BraVada Garrett-Akinsanya, "Growing Up without a Father: The Impact on Girls and Women," *Insight News*, accessed March 15, 2016, www.insightnews.com/2011/11/03/growing-up-without-a-father-the-impact-on-girls-and-women/.

13. John Rosemond, "Kids Aren't Special but Their Actions Are," *Journal Times*, October 17, 1999, www.journaltimes.com/lifestyles/kids-aren-t-special-but-their-actions-are/article_bff7d583-5685-514e-9bd7-5a5e8890df84.html.

14. Wikipedia, s.v. "image of God," accessed March 15, 2016, https://en.wikipedia.org/wiki/Image_of_God; and John Mark Comer, *Garden City: Work, Rest, and the Art of Being Human* (Grand Rapids, MI: Zondervan, 2015), 40.

DATING MYTH #3: I'M IN LOVE

1. A. P. Arnold, "Sex Chromosomes and Brain Gender," *Nature Reviews Neuroscience* 5, no. 9 (2004): 701–8.

2. Donna M. Werling and Daniel H. Geschwind, "Sex Differences in Autism Spectrum Disorders," *Current Opinion in Neurology* 26, no. 2 (2013), www.ncbi.nlm.nih.gov/pubmed/23406909, doi: 10.1097/WCO.0b013e32835ee548.

3. "Understanding Girls' Brains," PBS Parents, accessed March 15, 2016, www.pbs.org/parents/parenting/raising-girls/body-image-identity/understanding-girls-brains/.

4. "Romance Reader Statistics," Romance Writers of America, accessed March 15, 2016, www.rwa.org/p/cm/ld/fid=582.

5. "Best-Selling Books: The Annual Top 100," *USA Today*, June 21, 2011, http://usatoday30.usatoday.com/life/books/news/2009-01-14-top-100-titles_N.htm.

6. Helen Fisher, *Why We Love: The Nature and Chemistry of Romantic Love* (New York: Henry Holt, 2004), 73.

7. A. Aron et al., "Reward, Motivation, and Emotion Systems Associated with Early-Stage Intense Romantic Love," *Journal of Neurophysiology* 94, no. 1 (2005): 327–37.

8. S. L. Murray and J. G. Holmes, "A Leap of Faith? Positive Illusions in Romantic Relationships," *Personality and Social Psychology Bulletin* 23 (1997): 586–604.

9. Q. J. Pittman and S. J. Spencer, "Neurohypophysial Peptides: Gatekeepers in the Amygdala," *Trends in Endocrinology and Metabolism* 16, no. 8 (2005): 343–44.

10. First Corinthians 13:4–8 THE MESSAGE.

11. Andreas Bartels and Semir Zeki, "The Neural Basis of Romantic Love," *NeuroReport* 11, no. 17 (2000): 3829–34.

DATING MYTH #4: SEX WILL ENHANCE MY RELATIONSHIP

1. Tyler Charles, "The Secret Sexual Revolution," *Relevant*, February 20, 2012, www.relevantmagazine.com/life/relationship/features/28337-the-secret -sexual-revolution.

2. Wolfram Schultz, "Multiple Reward Signals in the Brain," *Nature Reviews Neuroscience* 1 (December 2000): 199–207.

3. Justin R. Garcia et al., "Sexual Hook-Up Culture," American Psychological Association, February 2013, www.apa.org/monitor/2013/02/ce-corner.aspx.

4. Amber N. V. Ruigrok et al., "A Meta-Analysis of Sex Differences in Human Brain Structure," *Neuroscience and Biobehavioral Reviews* 39 (2014): 34–50.

5. Jeanie Lerche Davis, "Activity of Brain May Explain Men's Sex Drive," WebMD, March 8, 2004, www.webmd.com/sex-relationships/news/20040308 /activity-of-brain-may-explain-mens-sex-drive.

6. David M. Buss et al., "International Preferences in Selecting Mates: A Study of 37 Cultures," *Journal of Cross-Cultural Psychology* 21 (1990): 5–47.

7. Buss, "International Preferences," 5–47.

8. Russell D. Clark III and Elaine Hatfield, "Gender Differences in Receptivity to Sexual Offers," *Journal of Psychology and Human Sexuality* 2, no. 1 (1989): 39–55.

9. Baleigh Scott, "Turns Out Women Don't Like Casual Sex as Much as Men— and That Isn't a Bad Thing," *Verily*, October 26, 2015, http://verilymag.com /2015/10/men-women-casual-sex-differences.

10. Edward O. Laumann, Anthony Paik, and Raymond C. Rosen, "Sexual Dysfunction in the United States: Prevalence and Predictors," *Journal of the American Medical Association* 281 (1999): 537–44.

11. Roy F. Baumeister, Kathleen R. Catanese, and Kathleen D. Vohs, "Is There a Gender Difference in Strength of Sex Drive? Theoretical Views, Conceptual Distinctions, and a Review of the Relevant Evidence," *Personality and Social Psychology Review* 5, no. 3 (2001): 242–73.

12. M. M. Lim and L. J. Young, "Vasopressin-Dependent Neural Circuits Underlying Pair Bond Formation in the Monogamous Prairie Vole," *Neuroscience* 125, no. 1 (2004): 35–45.

13. Howard N. Snyder, "Sexual Assault of Young Children as Reported to Law Enforcement: Victim, Incident, and Offender Characteristics," US Department of Justice, July 2000, www.bjs.gov/content/pub/pdf/saycrle.pdf.

14. Jennifer L. Truman and Michael Planty, "Criminal Victimization, 2011," US Department of Justice, October 2012, www.bjs.gov/content/pub/pdf/cv11.pdf.

15. Walt Larimore, "Poll Shows Sex within Marriage Is More Fulfilling," Family First, accessed March 15, 2016, www.imom.com/poll-shows-sex-within -marriage-is-more-fulfilling/#.VkKdmfmrSM8.

DATING MYTH #5: LOVE AND SEX ARE THE SAME

1. Massimo Marraffa, "Theory of Mind," Internet Encyclopedia of Philosophy, accessed March 16, 2016, www.iep.utm.edu/theomind/.

2. "Evolutionary Psychology," accessed March 16, 2016, www.epjournal.net/wp -content/uploads/EP05612631.pdf.

3. "Nine Differences between the Male and Female Brain," Brain Fitness for Life, May 12, 2015, www.brainfitnessforlife.com/9-differences-between-the-male -and-female-brain/.

4. Leonard Sax, "Gender Differences in the Sequence of Brain Development," Education.com accessed March 16, 2016, www.education.com/reference /article/Ref_Boys_Girls/.

5. Wikipedia, s.v. "Anna Creek Station," accessed March 16, 2016, https://en.wikipedia.org/wiki/Anna_creek_station.

6. Jeff Caldwell, "What Will a New Fence Cost This Year?," Agriculture.com, February 29, 2012, www.agriculture.com/news/livestock/what-will-a-new-fence -cost-this-year_3-ar22518.

DATING MYTH #6: SEX COMES WITHOUT CONSEQUENCES

1. "Facts on American Teens' Sources of Information about Sex," Guttmacher Institute, February 2012, www.guttmacher.org/pubs/FB-Teen-Sex-Ed.html.

2. "A Selective History of Sexuality Education in the United States," Advocates for Youth, accessed March 16, 2016, www.advocatesforyouth.org/serced/1859 -history-of-sex-ed.

3. "National Sexuality Education Standards," Future of Sexual Education, accessed March 16, 2016, www.futureofsexed.org/documents/josh-fose-standards-web.pdf.

4. "Key Statistics from the National Survey of Family Growth," Centers for Disease Control and Prevention, accessed March 16, 2016, www.cdc.gov /nchs/nsfg/key_statistics/s.htm#sexualactivity.

5. Sharon Jayson, "Teen Birth Rate Falls to Another Historic Low," *USA Today*, May 29, 2014, www.usatoday.com/story/news/nation/militaryintelligence /2014/05/29/birth-rate-teens/9670669/.

6. "Adolescent Fertility Rate," World Bank, accessed March 16, 2016, www.data.worldbank.org/indicator/SP.ADO.TFRT.

7. "Facts on American Teens' Sources," Guttmacher Institute, accessed December 3, 2015, www.guttmacher.org/pubs/FB-Teen-Sex-Ed.html.

8. Pamela K. Kohler, Lisa E. Manhart, and William E. Lafferty, "Abstinence-Only and Comprehensive Sex Education and the Initiation of Sexual Activity and Teen Pregnancy," *Journal of Adolescent Health* 42 (2008): 344–51, www.columbia.edu/cu/psychology/courses/3615/Readings/Kohler_2008.pdf.

9. Kathrin F. Stanger-Hall and David W. Hall, "Abstinence-Only Education and Teen Pregnancy Rates: Why We Need Comprehensive Sex Education in the US," Plos.org, October 14, 2011, http://journals.plos.org/plosone/article?id =10.1371/journal.pone.0024658#s1.

10. Dale Kunkel et al., "Sex on TV 4," Kaiser Family Foundation, November 2005, https://kaiserfamilyfoundation.files.wordpress.com/2013/01/sex-on-tv -4-full-report.pdf.

11. Daniel J. Siegel, "Pruning, Myelination, and the Remodeling Adolescent Brain," *Psychology Today*, February 4, 2014, www.psychologytoday.com /blog/inspire-rewire/201402/pruning-myelination-and-the-remodeling -adolescent-brain.

12. Beth Azar, "Oxytocin's Other Side," American Psychological Association, March 2011, www.apa.org/monitor/2011/03/oxytocin.aspx.

13. Rita Watson, "Oxytocin: The Love and Trust Hormone Can Be Deceptive," *Psychology Today*, October 14, 2013, www.psychologytoday.com/blog/love

-and-gratitude/201310/oxytocin-the-love-and-trust-hormone-can-be
-deceptive.

14. Linda Dillow and Dr. Juli Slattery, *Surprised by the Healer: Embracing Hope for Your Broken Story* (Chicago: Moody, 2016).

15. Steven Stosny, "Chains of Resentment," *Psychology Today*, September 9, 2011, www.psychologytoday.com/blog/anger-in-the-age-entitlement/201109 /chains-resentment.

16. "Post-Traumatic Embitterment Disorder: The Newest Mental Illness?," ScienceBlogs, June 2, 2009, www.scienceblogs.com/grrlscientist/2009/06/02 /posttraumatic-embitterment-dis/.

17. Donna Freitas, *The End of Sex: How Hookup Culture Is Leaving a Generation Unhappy, Sexually Unfulfilled, and Confused about Intimacy* (New York: Basic Books, 2013), 25.

18. Justin R. Garcia et al., "Sexual Hookup Culture: A Review," American Psychological Association, 2012, www.apa.org/monitor/2013/02/sexual -hookup-culture.pdf.

19. "When It Comes to College 'Hookups,' More Is Said Than Done," *University of Nebraska-Lincoln News Blog*, September 12, 2011, http://newsroom.unl .edu/blog/?p=737.

20. Freitas, *End of Sex*, 14.

21. American Sociological Association, "Study Challenges Popular Perception of New 'Hookup Culture' on College Campuses," ScienceDaily, August 13, 2013, www.sciencedaily.com/releases/2013/08/130813101814.htm.

22. Justin R. Garcia et al., "Sexual Hookup Culture," American Psychological Association, February 2013, www.apa.org/monitor/2013/02/ce-corner.aspx.

23. "FAQ: What Is 'Slut-Shaming'?," *Finally, a Feminism 101 Blog*, April 4, 2010, www.finallyfeminism101.wordpress.com/2010/04/04/what-is-slut-shaming/.

24. Rachel Pomerance Berl, "Making Sense of the Stats on Binge Drinking," *US News and World Report*, January 17, 2013, http://health.usnews.com/health -news/articles/2013/01/17/making-sense-of-the-stats-on-binge-drinking.

25. Jennifer L. Brown and Peter A. Vanable, "Alcohol Use, Partner Type, and Risky Sexual Behavior among College Students: Findings from an Event-Level Study," US National Library of Medicine, June 9, 2007, www.ncbi.nlm.nih .gov/pubmed/17611038.

26. "College Drinking," National Institute on Alcohol Abuse and Alcoholism, accessed March 16, 2016, http://pubs.niaaa.nih.gov/publications /CollegeFactSheet/CollegeFactSheet.pdf.

27. Garcia et al., "Sexual Hookup Culture."

28. Cynthia Perkins, "Understanding Alcohol Addiction," Alternatives for Alcoholism, accessed March 16, 2016, www.alternatives-for-alcoholism.com /alcohol-addiction.html.

29. Maia Szalavitz, "*DSM-5* Could Categorize 40 Percent of College Students as Alcoholics," *Time*, May 14, 2012, www.healthland.time.com/2012/05/14 /dsm-5-could-mean-40-of-college-students-are-alcoholics/.

30. Durham University, "Women Have Not Adapted to Casual Sex, Research Shows," ScienceDaily, June 26, 2008, www.sciencedaily.com/releases /2008/06/080625092023.htm.

31. Susan Kolod, "Is Hookup Regret More Common in Women?," *Psychology Today*, April 19, 2014, www.psychologytoday.com/blog/contemporary -psychoanalysis-in-action/201404/is-hookup-regret-more-common -in-women.

32. Garcia et al., "Sexual Hookup Culture."

33. Garcia et al., "Sexual Hookup Culture."

34. Anthony Paik, "Adolescent Sexuality and the Risk of Marital Dissolution," *Journal of Marriage and Family* 73 (April 2011): 472–85.

35. Anahad O'Connor, "The Claim: Women Get Drunk Faster Than Men," *New York Times*, August 16, 2005, www.nytimes.com/2005/08/16/health/the -claim-women-get-drunk-faster-than-men.html?_r=0.

36. Romans 12:2 THE MESSAGE.

37. Romans 12:2 NIV.

38. Paik, "Adolescent Sexuality," 472–85.

DATING MYTH #7: IT'S OKAY TO BREAK UP AND GET BACK TOGETHER

1. Louann Brizendine, *The Female Brain* (New York: Three Rivers, 2006), 75.

2. Brizendine, *Female Brain*, 40.

3. "Chronic Stress Puts Your Health at Risk," Mayo Clinic, accessed March 16, 2016, www.mayoclinic.org/healthy-lifestyle/stress-management/in-depth /stress/art-20046037.

4. "Bereishit—Genesis—Chapter 2," Chabad.org, accessed March 16, 2016, www.chabad.org/library/bible_cdo/aid/8166/jewish/Chapter-2.htm.

5. Doovie Jacoby, personal interview with author, July 15, 2015.

6. John Mark Comer, *Loveology: God. Love. Marriage. Sex. And the Never-Ending Story of Male and Female* (Grand Rapids, MI: Zondervan, 2013), 100.

DATING MYTH #8: HE WILL NEVER HIT ME AGAIN

1. "Dating Abuse Statistics," Loveisrespect.org, accessed March 16, 2016, www.loveisrespect.org/resources/dating-violence-statistics/.

2. "Teen Dating Violence," Centers for Disease Control and Prevention, accessed March 16, 2016, www.cdc.gov/violenceprevention/intimatepartnerviolence /teen_dating_violence.html.

3. Christine Ourada, personal interview with author, July 24, 2014.

4. "The Teen Brain: Still under Construction," National Institute of Mental Health, accessed March 16, 2016, www.nimh.nih.gov/health/publications /the-teen-brain-still-under-construction/index.shtml.

5. Louann Brizendine, *The Female Brain* (New York: Three Rivers, 2006), 42.

6. Brizendine, *Female Brain*, 42.

7. Shelley E. Taylor, "Tend and Befriend Theory," UCLA, accessed March 16, 2016, https://taylorlab.psych.ucla.edu/wp-content/uploads/sites/5/2014 /11/2011_Tend-and-Befriend-Theory.pdf.

8. Kenny Luck, "Making Marriage Work," Dr. John G. Kuna and Associates, June 10, 2015, www.drjohngkuna.com/blog/2228565/Making-Marriage -Work/1212356http://www.butler-bowdon.com/7-principles-making -marriage-work.

9. Personal interview, July 31, 2014.

10. "Daddyless Daughters: How to Establish Healthy Bonds with Men in Adulthood," Oprah.com, accessed March 16, 2016, www.oprah.com/oprahs-lifeclass /Daddyless-Daughters-How-to-Establish-Healthy-Bonds-with-Men-Video.

11. Stephen Chbosky, *The Perks of Being a Wallflower* (New York: MTV Books, 1999), 24.

12. "Domestic Violence and Abuse: Signs of Abuse and Abusive Relationships," HelpGuide.org, accessed March 16, 2016, www.helpguide.org/articles/abuse /domestic-violence-and-abuse.htm.

13. "Domestic (Intimate Partner) Violence Fast Facts," CNN, May 18, 2015, www.cnn.com/2013/12/06/us/domestic-intimate-partner-violence-fast-facts/.

14. Karen S. Peterson, "Studies Shatter Myth about Abuse," *USA Today*, June 22, 2003, http://usatoday30.usatoday.com/news/health/2003-06-22-abuse-usat _x.htm.

DATING MYTH #9: A REBOUND RELATIONSHIP IS JUST WHAT I NEED

1. "Ann Landers," AZ Quotes, accessed March 16, 2016, www.azquotes.com /quote/167601.

2. "Thanksgiving III," *The Middle*, ABC (November 23, 2011).

DATING MYTH #10: SERIAL DATING AND LIVING TOGETHER WILL HELP ME STAY MARRIED

1. Wikipedia, s.v. "salmon run," accessed March 16, 2016, https://en.wikipedia .org/wiki/Salmon_run.

2. University of Virginia, "Social Indicators of Marital Health and Well-Being," State of Our Unions, 2011, www.stateofourunions.org/2011/social _indicators.php.

3. "Pathways to Adulthood and Marriage: Teenagers' Attitudes, Expectations, and Relationship Patterns," US Department of Health and Human Services, October 1, 2008, www.aspe.hhs.gov/hsp/08/pathways2adulthood/ch3.shtml.

4. Judy Kilpatrick, "What Are the Effects of High School Students Having a Boyfriend or Girlfriend?," Global Post, accessed March 16, 2016, http://everydaylife.globalpost.com/effects-high-school-students-having -boyfriend-girlfriend-6709.html.

5. Casey E. Copen, Kimberly Daniels, and William D. Mosher, "First Premarital Cohabitation in the United States: 2006–2010 National Survey of Family Growth," *National Health Statistics Reports*, April 4, 2013, www.cdc.gov/nchs /data/nhsr/nhsr064.pdf.

6. Robert Hughes Jr., "What Is the Real Divorce Rate in the US?," Huffington Post, May 25, 2011, www.huffingtonpost.com/robert-hughes/what-is-the-real -divorce-_b_785045.html.

7. Sharon Sassler, "The Higher Risks of Cohabitation," *New York Times*, December 20, 2010, www.nytimes.com/roomfordebate/2010/12/19/why-remarry/the -higher-risks-of-cohabitation.

8. Eleanor Barkhorn, "Getting Married Later Is Great for College-Educated Women," *Atlantic Monthly*, March 15, 2013, www.theatlantic.com/sexes /archive/2013/03/getting-married-later-is-great-for-college-educated -women/274040/.

9. "FAQ: Facts and Statistics, Love and Relationships," Kinsey Institute, accessed March 16, 2016, www.kinseyinstitute.org/resources/FAQ.html#number.

10. Michelle Castillo, "CDC: More Women Choosing Cohabitation before Marriage," CBS News, April 4, 2013, www.cbsnews.com/news/cdc-more -women-choosing-cohabitation-before-marriage/.

11. S. R. H. Beach and F. D. Fincham, "Spontaneous Remission of Marital Discord: A Simmering Debate with Profound Implications for Family Psychology," *Family Psychologist* 19 (2003): 11–13.

12. "Divorce Statistics," Divorcestatistics.org, accessed March 16, 2016, www.divorcestatistics.org/.

13. Sharon Jayson, "Social Change Accelerates across Generations," *USA Today*, February 26, 2014, www.usatoday.com/story/news/nation/2014/02/26 /arizona-gay-rights-brewer-marijuana/5812997/?AID=10709313&PID =6152146&SID=84xctcwtc69p.

14. Meg Jay, "The Downside of Cohabiting before Marriage," *New York Times*, April 14, 2012, www.nytimes.com/2012/04/15/opinion/sunday/the -downside-of-cohabiting-before-marriage.html?pagewanted=all&_r=0.

15. Catherine Rampell, "Marriage Is for Rich People," *New York Times*, February 6, 2012, www.economix.blogs.nytimes.com/2012/02/06 /marriage-is-for-rich-people/?_r=0.

16. Anita Jose, Daniel K. O'Leary, and Anne Moyer, "Does Premarital Cohabitation Predict Subsequent Marital Stability and Marital Quality? A Meta-Analysis," *Journal of Marriage and Family* 72 (February 2010): 105–16.

17. Jay Teachman, "Premarital Sex, Premarital Cohabitation, and the Risk of Subsequent Marital Dissolution among Women," *Journal of Marriage and Family* 65 (May 2003): 444–55.

18. Ed Stetzer, "Marriage, Divorce, and the Church: What Do the Stats Say, and Can Marriage Be Happy?," *Christianity Today*, February 14, 2014, www.christianitytoday.com/edstetzer/2014/february/marriage-divorce -and-body-of-christ-what-do-stats-say-and-c.html.

19. Robert E. Rector et al., "The Harmful Effects of Early Sexual Activity and Multiple Sexual Partners among Women: A Book of Charts," Heritage Foundation, June 23, 2003, https://s3.amazonaws.com/thf_media/2003 /pdf/wm303.pdf.

20. Jenny Hope, "Marriage, the Key to a Better Life: Study Finds Tying the Knot Means Improved Health and Longer Life Expectancy," *Daily Mail*, January 28, 2011, www.dailymail.co.uk/femail/article-1351287/Marriage-key-better-life -Study-finds-tying-knot-means-improved-health-longer-life-expectancy.html.

21. Sharon Sassler, "The Higher Risks of Cohabitation," *New York Times*, December 20, 2010, www.nytimes.com/roomfordebate/2010/12/19 /why-remarry/the-higher-risks-of-cohabitation.

22. W. Bradford Wilcox, "Suffer the Little Children: Cohabitation and the Abuse of America's Children," Witherspoon Institute, April 22, 2011, www.thepublicdiscourse.com/2011/04/3181/.

23. Jenny Tyree, "The Truth about Domestic Violence in Marital versus Cohabitational Relationships," CitizenLink, June 14, 2010, www.citizenlink .com/2010/06/14/the-truth-about-domestic-violence-in-marital-versus -cohabitational-relationships/.